MEMOS TO MANAGEMENT

MEMOS TO MANAGEMENT

A DECLARATION
OF INDEPENDENCE
FOR PEOPLE IN
BIG BUSINESS

Frank A. Armstrong

STEIN AND DAY/*Publishers*/New York

First published in 1974
Copyright © 1974 by Frank A. Armstrong
Library of Congress Catalog Card No. 73-92188
All rights reserved
Designed by David Miller
Printed in the United States of America
Stein and Day/*Publishers*/Scarborough House,
Briarcliff Manor, N.Y. 10510
ISBN 0-8128-1691-9

To Dorothy, Mark, Christine and Michael . . . who are my main business.

CONTENTS

PREFACE

This nation cannot live without big business. Anyone who refuses to recognize that fact is living in a fantasy world. He is looking for a magic potion to reverse his maturity and make him a child again. We must accept the idea of living and working with big and complex organizations which, after all, have made this country what it is today: the most powerful industrial nation in the world.

But big business is presently misusing a great national resource: its most enterprising and energetic people.

This book is for people in big business who want it to continue to make an irreplaceable contribution to American life.

It is also for those people who refuse to join or are about to quit a big business because it no longer offers an opportunity for fulfillment, excitement, and a useful contribution to modern life.

It will describe those aspects of big business

that are demoralizing its best people and tell what can be done to stop this waste of invaluable human potential. It will offer concrete proposals for essential change. Some may at first appear wild-eyed. Others, while desirable, may appear unattainable. But what I offer is the direction and nature of changes that must be made.

The business system in which we live today has become increasingly vulnerable to critics who clamor for the break-up of big business or its regulation by a federal agency. If big business managers do not in the near future implement some of my proposals themselves they will find that the system's hardening arteries and softening underbelly have made it an irresistible target for forces that could destroy it.

Properly armed with the right ideas, all levels of management—young, old, at the top, in the middle—can effect these critical changes. I respectfully submit this book as an arsenal in their battle.

It obviously does not contain all that can or should be done. But after long experience and careful thought, I am confident that what I do propose will work.

I'm in business now, president of Moxie Industries Inc., and have been all my working life. I have worked with hundreds of top and middle management men in a wide variety of industries from pharmaceuticals to computers, insurance to catering, automotive manufacturing to communications. Because I have not spent my business career with one or two big companies, I am able to step back and give an objective view of big business today. My own company, Moxie, has grown from a small to a medium-sized business, and hopefully will be a big business before too long. For the purpose of this book, my experience is my most important credential.

A list of companies I have learned from:

Allied Chemical
American Home
American Motors
Anchor Hocking
Avon
Brunswick
Buick
Burlington
C.B.S.
Chesebrough-Pond's
Chrysler
Coca-Cola
Colgate
Corn Products
Cowles Communications
Del Monte
Dow Chemical
Du Pont
Flintkote
Ford
GMC Truck
General Foods

General Mills
Goodyear
Hilton Hotels
Heublein
IBM
I.T.T.
John Hancock
Jonathan Logan
Kinney National Service
L.T.V.
Magnavox
Maytag
Mead
Miles Laboratories
Revlon
Schenley
Scott Paper
Simmons
Sperry Hutchinson
Sun Oil
Milliken
Moxie Industries, Inc.
NCR
Nabisco
National Lead
Owens-Corning Fiberglass
J. C. Penney
Pepsico
Philco
RCA
Standard Oil of Ohio
Standard Oil of New Jersey

J. P. Stevens
Swift
Time Inc.
Warner-Lambert
Westinghouse

MEMO 1

BIG BUSINESS: THE GHOST TOWN OF TOMORROW?

Big business is under attack from some very articulate critics, from an ever-growing federal government, from intensifying international competition, and most damagingly, from many management people who want no part of big business as it is operating today.

In recent years, what with Nader, Townsend, Galbraith, and the rise of the ecology movement, it is easy to conclude that because a company is big, it's bad. At the same time, it is obvious to any responsible observer that we can't reverse ourselves: big business is here to stay. After all, big business has been tremendously successful in the last thirty years.

But what about the next thirty years?

I believe there is a critical need to change the way big companies manage people if big business is to continue to thrive. That's what this book is about. And you better believe there is a real problem.

When you see survey figures that indicate

only twenty-three per cent of college graduates want to work for a big company (in contrast to forty-four per cent of high school graduates) you can believe there is a problem. In fact, at the college level, seventy-one per cent of those students who opt for business careers would rather work for a small company or for themselves than in a big business. This is a complete reversal of the situation in the mid-fifties, when eighty-five per cent of all college graduates opted for a career in big business.

What people want today is a feeling of accomplishment. They also want pleasant working conditions and enjoyable work, but, most important, they want to take pride in what they do. They are not interested in short hours, fancy titles, achieving status, or not working at all. They are entirely ready and willing to work hard, but they want to feel they are achieving something worthwhile. In big business they feel their functions are fractionated and the sense of accomplishment is minor, and this discontent is *not* the product of media criticism. It has been developing for several generations.

Young potential management people don't want to become pieces of corporate baggage moved around from place to place, from time to time, at the whim of the corporation. In fact, over sixty per cent of those aspiring to a career in business state they don't want to take a job if it means moving a number of times. If you are with a big company now, you may say, "Well, that's because they really don't want to work and they won't show loyalty to the company." But, in fact, what these people are saying is that the other aspects of their lives, family and community for example, are also very important and not to be ignored, and when you move around a lot, real problems can develop in these areas.

Many middle management men already in big business are not happy either. They feel restricted and confined and left out. Representative are two bright young engineers who left a big electronics company to start their own small business, making electronic and audio components. "If we hadn't left," one of them said, "we would have drowned."

What's their basic gripe? Overspecialization. Business has become very complex. As a result, jobs, or functions, have been divided and subdivided again and again. When you get a man who is responsible for handling one-fiftieth of the basic function, he gets to feel like he is one-fiftieth of a man. It is almost impossible for him to believe he is responsible for any final results. His sense of accomplishment is at the two per cent level. That's why so many really top quality middle management people are moving to smaller companies or starting their own small companies. In a smaller company, a person's total function may not be as large and as complex and as important, but what he has responsibility for is more significant; and then, when he gets the job done and sees the results, the results can be their own reward.

Many middle management people today aren't interested in the traditional company rituals used to keep them "in their proper place." For example, I know of a field sales management man who was transferred to headquarters, a big promotion for him. The day he moved in he was given a small, private office with a window—only to be told shortly that there had been a mistake: his rank did not entitle him to a window. He was then moved to a slightly larger office, but he had to share it with two other men. He had taken with him from the first office a metal-trimmed blotter. A few days later, one of the senior executives saw the blotter on his desk and told him that he ought to give it back because it was an "executive blotter."

The security offered by many big companies also no longer has the appeal it used to. Few people ever get fired, but the environment is non-innovative and non-competitive, and this is not what people want to do whether they are just starting their careers or are energetic, ambitious men already in mid-stride.

There are a lot of people dropping out today and they are not just the kids in school. Big business is getting more and more of its share of dropouts. Many of these people are not concerned about changing the system or overthrowing it, but simply with turning their backs on it and on its values and on its organizational trappings. They are rejecting what might best be called "Corporate America" and its world of impersonal decisions, of bureaucracy, of steady income. Some of these people are going back to nature, to farming, or to the sea. Few of these dropouts were converted by colleagues or associates, and few of them have taken colleagues with them when they left. The decision to leave the big organization doesn't just happen; it emerges over a period of time to men who found their jobs frustrating and, at best, the work boring and meaningless. Expressions of boredom recur in their conversations. They yearn for more fulfilling work than they have had as well-paid hirelings of one big company or another.

Some big business dropouts are in their forties and fifties; men who, through diligent decades of career building, managed to set aside substantial savings and who in mid-step decided that their careers were of little consequence and that life is too short to spend it doing the wrong things for the wrong reasons. Some say that they were influenced by the distaste that their children, both grown up and those still at home, exhibited for the parents' way of life.

Many believe that when you give most of your waking hours to a big company it owns you. Even if you have a sense of well being or opportunity, you are denying yourself the freedom to change and to do something radically different. Doing the same thing every day for decades is deadening. Monoculture is bad in farming and it's bad in living. Fifty acres of land can't stand up to being planted with nothing but wheat. It could be argued that some of these people have failed in big business and have not been successful, and it's true. But a lot of the dropouts have been very successful. When they leave, some of their former business associates think, as one man put it, "I was out of my mind."

Sun Oil Company is an example of a company making changes. They are doing away with time-honored practices and attitudes and they are trying to get rid of the incredible duplication of effort in so many departments. They are decentralizing and they are giving executives at all levels more authority and more responsibility. The headquarter's executive group that handled field operations largely by remote control has been broken up. Three major operating segments of the company are now under the control of vice presidents, each of whom has his own team of men. Sun Oil has recognized that the need to give more people more autonomy and opportunity to control their activities that contribute to the success of their own operations.

Look at it this way. If the middle management of a company is not productive and not happy, then the best of these people are going to leave, and for that big corporation there is going to be a shortage of top executive talent in the next ten to fifteen years.

Alfred North Whitehead has said, "Any groove of abstraction is bound to be an inadequate way of describing reality." For this reason, I get specific about problems and solutions in this book. It is obvious that no big business is perfect. It is obvious that most can change and improve. I use specific examples of problems and solutions because I know that it is so much more effective to deal in specific rather than abstract terms.

MEMO 2

IF YOU'RE SO RICH, WHY AREN'T YOU HAPPY?

Today American industry produces twice the goods of all European industry combined. Right now American industry produces two and one-half times more than the Soviet Union, which has a far greater population than the U.S.A. American industry produces one third of the total production of all other countries in the world. Americans have achieved this with about seven per cent of the surface of the globe and something less than six per cent of its total population.

Americans also consume one third of the world's total production of energy. One third of all the world's highways are in the United States. Half of the passenger miles flown every year are flown by Americans on U.S.A. airlines. Two trucks of every five on the roads of the world are American made and American based.

American technology and finance and management skills have raised per capita production in the United States to forty per cent above that of the next highest country, Sweden. The per capita production is sixty per cent above Germany and seventy per cent above Great Britain. The driving force behind this productivity is American big business. The combined profits of the ten biggest companies in France and Britain and Germany are two billion dollars. The profits of General Motors alone exceed this. From 1960 to 1970 American corporations doubled the annual total of their investments in their own businesses. They did this, in large part, out of their earnings rather than from bank loans. During the last ten years the gross profits of American corporations have grown every year, and American companies are plowing this profit back into business.

Of the ninety companies in the world doing more than one billion dollars a year in sales, only thirty are not American owned. In other words, America has more than half of the big industrial giants, with their capacity for vast commercial and technological development. Let's take a step down to companies doing more than five hundred million dollars in sales a year. In 1960 the United States had over a hundred such companies. All of Europe had about thirty, and the rest of the world, around twenty-five. By 1972 the United States had over one hundred fifty companies in this category. Europe had moved up to around fifty, and the rest of the world to the same level. It is clear that big businesses are growing bigger in the United States, and that we are getting more of them.

When we look at the figures on the basis of share of world production, again the U. S. dominates:

Industry	U.S.A.	Rest of the World
Machinery	70%	30%
Autos	75%	25%
Oil	70%	30%
Electronics	70%	30%
Chemicals	60%	40%

In computers, such a key part of technological growth, IBM alone is currently doing about sixty per cent of the business in the entire world. When our other producers in the field are added to this figure, the total comes to over seventy per cent.

American business is more profitable than business in the rest of the world, and this higher level of profit is largely due to big business. For example, when compared to the Common Market, American business had in 1960 a six per cent profit margin, and in the next ten years this percentage increased to around seven per cent. At the same time, the *profit margins* for Common Market business in 1960 were around three and one-half per cent and they have decreased slightly in the last ten years.

The large companies of this country have

been able to develop, because of their size, the full scientific and technological potential available to them. In this connection they have worked closely with American universities, which have in turn pushed these big companies into new areas of development and new areas of growth. Big business in this country has worked closely with government on many projects, and while this is criticized in some circles the results in overall productivity and economic gain have been considerable.

The U.S.A. and Japan and, possibly, Sweden are the only countries that will by 1985 enter a post-industrial era, in which electronic communications and computers will change the character of the economy from being production oriented to being marketing oriented. At the same time, Europe and Russia will remain in an industrial form of economy; and of course the rest of the countries, particularly South America and the Orient, will be largely pre-industrial. The U.S.A. now has a vast lead in space electronics, chemicals, computers, automobiles, and atomic energy.

What does all this mean to us? We can agree that big business has been doing a great job in production and growth. At the same time, we have to recognize that within this country a major movement has developed, particularly with younger people, that is opposed to big business. Statistics indicate fewer and fewer young men want to join big business and criticism of big business increases daily. But what is in fact proposed as an alternative?

A few romantics suggest we go back to an earlier period in which small businesses dominated the economy which is, of course, completely unrealistic.

Another alternative is to break up big business. We have had in this country many, many antitrust laws, and they have been tough. But they have been only spasmodically enforced. The truth is that antitrust legislation in this country has failed to keep up with the rapidly evolving economy. None of the major antitrust laws of 1890, 1894, 1914, 1936, 1938, and 1950 was effective in slowing down the pace of growth and consolidation of big business. Despite the establishment of a strong Federal Trade Commission to monitor and enforce the law, little has been done to slow the movement of American industries toward bigger and bigger units.

Another group of critics suggests that the federal government have much more control of big business: specifically, federal chartering of corporations would replace state chartering. The federal charter could include specific controls which would cover the whole impact of the corporation on society. With this system, the federal government would know about corporate product development and new product research investments. Consumers would be able to go to the federal government with a complaint about a big corporation, and the federal government would then act. There would be a whole host of new requirements for shareholder rights. It would be easier to nominate directors and, possibly, publicly elect a portion of all boards.

You can see what all this would lead to. If in fact there is a problem today with bigness in business, can you imagine the size and scope of the federal organization that would have to be put in place to "manage" business for the federal government? If it is true that bigness by itself has a number of inherent problems, then through such a plan we would add another huge organization within our total economic structure.

None of these alternatives will work: the revival of small businesses, the breakup of big business through legislation, or the control of big business by big government. At the same time, major changes are required in big business. These are changes in operational methods and in personnel relations.

If big business has been imaginative and innovative in technological and market development, then surely it is capable of imaginative innovation when it comes to developing a new environment for its management people.

MEMO 3

IS THE WORK ETHIC ON THE SKIDS?

In the mid-eighteen hundreds and particularly in the period following the Civil War, American business began expanding rapidly beyond the proprietorship and small business stage. Individual companies grew in size and the first indications of organization complexity and bureaucracy developed. If business leaders in those days had an operational philosophy, it came directly from the Protestant or Work Ethic. The Protestant Work Ethic gave to the proprietor and entrepreneur a specific and particular attitude and style in management. I might add at this point that the Work Ethic, as it affected American business, certainly did not and does not apply only to Protestants; it could just as well have been called the Jewish Ethic; and in many ways the Jewish people in business have been the most effective users of this management attitude.

At a Yale University graduation in 1908, the Protestant Work Ethic was defined by banker Henry Clews:

"*Survival of Fittest*: You may start in business with your feet on the bottom rung of the ladder; it rests with you to acquire the strength to climb to the top. You can do so if you have the will and the force to back you. There is always plenty of room at the top. . . . Success comes to the man who tries to compel success to yield to him. Cassius spoke well to Brutus when he said, 'The fault is not in our stars, dear Brutus, that we are underlings, but in our natures.' "

The Protestant Work Ethic produced a hard-boiled approach to management, and it was incomplete, of course, without companion assurance that the success produced was moral as well as practical.

"Under this free system of government, whereby individuals are free to get a living or to pursue wealth as each chooses, the usual result is competition. Obviously, then, competition really means industrial freedom. Thus, anyone may choose his own trade or profession, or, if he does not like it, he may change. He is free to work hard or not; he may make his own bargains and set his price upon his labor or his products. By dint of greater effort or superior skill, or by intelligence, if he can make better wages, he is free to live better, just as his neighbor is free to follow his example and to learn to excel him in turn. If anyone has a genius for making and managing money, he is free to exercise his genius, just as another is free to handle his tools. . . . If an individual enjoys his money, gained by energy and successful effort, his neighbors are urged to work the harder, that they and their children may have the same enjoyment."

The Protestant Work Ethic was a positive and optimistic one. It allowed everyone to believe that pursuing his self-interest improved the lot of all, and that hard work could eventually produce a "heaven on earth."

It is perfectly clear that the Protestant Work Ethic helped make capitalism the success that it is today, and it helped make big business possible in the process.

The Protestant Work Ethic also created an attitude and style of management that was driving, tough, demanding, strict, and that in effect used fear as its major source of motivation. "You do it, or else!" best expressed the owner's or the manager's attitude. *Under the Protestant Work Ethic, respect for authority is the central and absolutely indispensable means of management control.* This basic premise of organization is in virtually every textbook on the theory of management available today. The structure of the organization reflects a hierarchy of authoritative relationships. The terms "up" and "down" in such a structure refer to the scale of authority. Most of the other current principles of organizations (such as unity of control where many men report to one man) are derived from the authoritarian principle of management.

By World War I, private enterprise had discovered the benefits of public ownership and ever since it has increased at a rapid rate.

As far as management was concerned, a major change took place. The professional manager came into being, often replacing an entrepreneur-owner. In many cases the professional manager was hand-picked by the owner to "carry on" the business for him. But the professional manager, though often not even a major stockholder, employed the same methods of management used by the proprietor. He has run big business as if the "Big Boss" were still operating. He may not have ownership on his side but he does have the size of the organization or the department that he runs to support his power and to perpetuate the authoritarian techniques of management developed by his predecessor.

Today, however, the social and economic milieu of the United States has been transformed and management can no longer rely on an inborn respect for authority among its personnel.

The Protestant Work Ethic no longer propels the individual forward and upward in the pursuit of success. Without this drive, the individual employee cannot be goaded by fear of losing a chance for promotion or being demoted or fired. Psychologically, he is no longer as dependent on the company as he once was. If he doesn't like it he leaves, and if he doesn't like what he sees in big business he doesn't enter big business. As dependence decreases, the capacity for management to use authoritarian control decreases in direct proportion. Over the last thirty years, dependence on the organization by the individual has decreased steadily, and in the process authoritarian control has continued to lose effectiveness. We are now at the point in big business where dependence is almost nonexistent and the interdependence of top managers on the sub-manager is mandatory. Dependence must become a two-way street.

MEMO 4

THE BELLOWING BOSS: IS ANYBODY LISTENING?

The type of man who manages big business is changing. In simplest terms, the bright, aggressive, energetic, power-driven, *mean son-of-a-bitch* is on his way out. The man who looks upon himself as the "Big Boss" is not going to make it in the future. Why?

Didn't this type of manager help build big business to where it is today? Of course. But we have a new world now and people have changed. What they want out of their work and what they expect in their relationship with a big organization are quite different from what people wanted twenty or thirty years ago. As a result, management must change. This becomes more obvious when we consider the very size and complexity of big business organizations. They require a wide variety of disciplines to function effectively. This means, of course, that more people must have more responsibility and authority for the organization to be effective. In the classical organization there was one boss in a pyramid-type structure, and, theoretically at least, he knew all and told all. Behind the attitude of authoritarian control are some very basic assumptions about human nature and human behavior.

The first assumption is that the average person really doesn't like to work and, given an opportunity, will do everything he can to avoid it. This assumption has very deep roots. At all management levels in big business, there is the constant grading and evaluation of managers that specifies those who are "hard workers" and really put in the hours against those who tend to featherbed. There is also an emphasis on rewards reflecting an underlying belief that this is the only way to counteract the natural tendency not to work as hard as possible.

The second basic premise is that, because people don't like to work, even the promise of reward is insufficient. Most people must also be coerced and controlled and directed and threatened to get them to do an effective job. People may accept their rewards for doing a job and then come right back and want additional ones to continue the effort. Therefore, only the threat of punishment will perpetuate a high level of performance.

The third basic premise is that the average person actually prefers to be directed and wishes to avoid responsibility because he or she has relatively little ambition. In the final analysis, what people really want out of the big organization is security, which is why they chose to join a big company in the first place. These assumptions about the mediocrity of most people becomes clear when you talk to top management about the problems they are having with the people who work for them.

In the authoritative style of all too many big company managers, the major weapon of control is fear. The manager lets people know that if they don't do what he wants them to do, he won't give them more money; he won't promote them; and, if the problem is severe enough, he will fire them. When he wants to get people to do more than they are doing, he uses money on the end of a stick as the key part of his motivation.

All too often, the management man in big business considers the *manipulation* of the people under him a key and fundamental part of his job. If this manipulation requires some shading of truth, so be it. Most often, however, it takes the form of lack of directness or secrecy in dealing with people under him. The manager often withholds fundamental information to maintain control. Unlike the original entrepreneur-owner, today's management man doesn't have the ultimate sway of ownership; but within prescribed limits he can muster the full power of the organization behind him, and this in effect gives him what he considers to be absolute control. Take a look, for example, at the way people are moved from area to area. This disrupts personal life but is justified because it is "good for the corporation". Besides, the move represents a "promotion" and usually more money. Notice how many times a man must accept a promotion, must take on added responsibility, and must make a move if necessary, or be marked within the company as a "no go," as a man who is not totally committed to the company and therefore should not be considered again for promotion.

Bonus plans are still rife throughout big business. Studies show that most bonuses are given for company or division or regional performance in sales or production or profit. They are established ahead of time as incentives to get people to work harder. Yet the truth is, it is highly debatable whether such bonuses do get people to work harder, and it is highly debatable whether the results achieved are because of individual or group performance, or just because the increase in business or profit was going to occur anyway. The very size of big business means there is often a tremendous lag between action and result in sales and profit. For example, in the automotive industry, men are rewarded for sales increases that are the direct result of actions and plans made by their predecessors five, six, and eight years before.

The Protestant Ethic type of management man is out of date. He no longer can attract the kind of talent that is necessary to maintain the strength of big business. He cannot generate teamwork in the variety of disciplines needed in big business today. This management man stifles men, restricts creative effort, holds back new ideas and new approaches to problem solving. This management man does not have the ability to motivate the kind of people who should be coming into big business today but all too often are rejecting big business because of the stifling effect that authoritarian management produces.

What can be done about the out-of-date management man? We can retrain him to use modern leadership methods of management. Or—and I don't mean to appear to be autocratic about this but it is a matter of survival—if the manager can't be trained to use new methods of leadership, *he has got to go!*

MEMO 5

PROFIT BEFORE PEOPLE:
A STONE AGE APPROACH?

Often a lag occurs between the time a new idea is needed and the time it actually arrives. The hierarchical structure has been used in business for a long time and has lasted long beyond its period of usefulness. For too long, management at all levels of big business have held on to the ideas of hierarchical management:

- The idea of the boss as one who is all-knowing and all-powerful and in absolute control.
- The idea of motivating with money.
- The idea of motivating through fear.
- The idea of manipulation through the control of information.
- The idea of using the very bigness of big business to maintain control.

This approach to managing won't work today. It is too simple-minded, and really just a step away from the most primitive form of management: control through physical force.

Today more knowledge about what motivates and stimulates people is available and we have to make use of it. The very affluence that big business has helped to produce means that many of the material and basic needs of people are already fulfilled or assumed. More important in motivation than these material needs are the ego needs of people.

It is clear that the typical hierarchical and classical organization structure in pyramid form is no longer workable; it is too clumsy. The pyramid for the average big business has become far too big. The base is far too broad and the distance from top to bottom is incredibly far. This is the reason, of course, that people in big business complain about the lack of movement, the lack of feeling that they are contributing to results in a meaningful way, and the certainty that, as individuals, they are not particularly important or meaningful to the gigantic pyramid.

At the same time, it is clear that forays into "round table" type of organization structure have not been practical and workable. All of the people can't be at the same level and all can't have an equal voice in management. Full participatory democracy, in its purest form, will not serve big business well. There has to be a head of the table; there has to be someone who, in the final analysis, makes the final decisions.

Instead of one gigantic pyramid, what is needed is a bunch of smaller pyramids:

pyramids that have the capacity and the authority and the responsibility to function on their own. Smaller pyramids that make it possible for more people to understand what it is that they are working on and to feel a sense of accomplishment when a job is done. Smaller pyramids that, because of improved communication, permit something that is closer to participatory democracy.

It should be noted that the idea of breaking down the single, gigantic pyramid into a series of smaller pyramids is already being done in some big companies, and that the significant point is not something you can draw on a wall and say, "That's how the company is organized," in order to display the total organizational structure. It is the change in *attitude* that is required to establish the smaller pyramid concept of organization structure. The "organization chart" in any form, for a gigantic pyramid or for many smaller pyramids is, at best, an artificial device and does not really give a true picture of how a big business functions. When the big pyramid is broken up into a group of smaller pyramids, the significant change is not on the organization chart but in the attitude of the people working within the company.

Big business must change attitudes because it is clear that people *do* have a capacity to exercise a very high degree of imagination and ingenuity and creativity in solving the problems of big business *if they are given the right environment in which to do this.* In all too many cases, people are stifled by the giant pyramid, or by routine work, or by a lack of vision, and do not use their full potential. This means the money invested in these people is not returning a full measure of productivity.

The social scientists know now that, under the right conditions, people do not dislike work, but welcome it as they do rest or play. Given the right conditions, work can be a source of considerable satisfaction. It is only when work is *demanded* under a hierarchical organizational structure and when fear is used as a major source of motivation that people don't like to work. In these conditions they want only to leave precisely at closing time. They look forward to the weekend as the only satisfying and rewarding time in a long week.

Fear is used at management levels in big business in many ways. There is the fear produced by competitive job pressures, the fear produced by events and situations beyond the individual's control, the fear produced by an uncertain future, the fear produced by the oppression of the hierarchical organization.

But the fact is, people *will* exercise self-direction and self-control in the service of the company without fear being used; people will work creatively and imaginatively and productively towards company objectives *when they receive from their work a feeling of satisfaction and a sense of accomplishment*. Doing the job becomes a reward in itself. Achieving a significant goal becomes a reward in itself.

People do not shun responsibility; they

want responsibility. The avoidance of responsibility and the lack of ambition are generally the consequences of a poor working environment, rather than any inherent and basic human characteristics. Of course, perfect integration of company goals and individual goals is not a realistic objective. What is needed is a degree of integration in which the individual can achieve his goals *best* by directing his efforts toward the goals of the company.

Let's look at the ego needs of the person. First, there is the individual's self-esteem. He wants to feel that what he is doing and how he is doing it are important and that he can take pride in what he is doing. To achieve this, he must have a clear understanding of what his job is and how it contributes to the company's goals and objectives. Then, when the company achieves its goals and objectives, the individual can rightfully take pride in what has been achieved.

An individual wants and seeks a degree of autonomy. Not total autonomy. No man is an island, and everyone has to report to someone. He needs to feel he is treated as an independent individual. You must give him a job to do and express confidence in his capacity to do that job on his own.

In addition, there is the need for a sense of achievement. A man or woman must feel that he is doing something worthwhile and he must be able to see clearly what he has accomplished. Over the years, the effect of this feeling of achievement can be measured by an increase in his confidence and ability to perform higher and higher level functions; the expansion of knowledge in a sub-discipline to the total discipline, for example.

To sum up, big business must help the person to look at his individual relation to his work and to the company in a positive way, and to realize that all the requirements for self-esteem can be found in that relation.

One other important aspect of egoistic needs relates, not to how the person sees himself, but to how others see him, and to his reputation, not only in the company, but in the community. There has to be recognition of accomplishment on the part of the company and this should not be something that is grudgingly handed down from above but, instead, delivered eye to eye and handshake to handshake.

Finally, the person wants respect from his fellow workers, and he doesn't want it just because he is in a position of power but because it is deserved. He wants it because he is recognized for what he has done and can do in his own particular discipline.

The egoistic needs of the individual are satisfied through his self-fulfillment. When a person realizes he is making maximum use of his talent and intelligence and energy, he feels self-fulfillment. When he realizes that his full potentialities are being recognized, he feels self-fulfillment. When he believes without question that, in the job that he is in and in the company that he is part of, there is an opportunity for continued self-development, then he feels self-fulfillment. When he feels that he is being creative, in the broadest sense of the term, and developing creative solutions to the problems, there is self-fulfillment.

The tactical possibilities within conventional management attitudes in the hierarchical organization have pretty much been exploited. The new attitude for big business toward people demands that big business have much more confidence in the capacity and ability of individuals for self-direction. It demands that big business design jobs with individuals in mind so that the goals, both business and personal, of the particular person can be considered in the definition of goals for the company.

This new approach requires big business to wake up and recognize that there is a high degree of imagination and ingenuity and creativity available when the proper environment is created. This new attitude requires that management no longer make fulfilling materialistic needs of primary importance. Instead, the egoistic needs of people should come first, paradoxically, if big business is to sustain its present prosperity.

IS CONFORMITY
BOXING IN BIG BUSINESS?

Much has been written about the conformity
and uniformity of behavior of the executive in
big business. In hundreds of articles and dozens of books, the practices have been
analyzed, evaluated, and in many cases
severely criticized. And yet with all the criticism, it is clear today that many of these practices of conformity and uniformity are still
pursued diligently. Here, in the form of quota-
tions, are many that I have been exposed to in
my contact with big business over the years:

"I don't care what you say about his
ability . . . he is forty pounds overweight and that
tells me all I need to know."

"The truth is, a white shirt and a dark suit are
more businesslike."

"He's a painter on the weekends?"

"It may seem silly to you, Mary . . . but you
really do have to get on with their wives."

"If they don't want me to make coffee in my
office . . . I won't make coffee in my office."

"The point I am trying to make is that there shouldn't be any questions about it . . . the corporation does come first."

"Actually, I make it a habit never to talk politics."

"You shouldn't be so opinionated in those meetings . . . you never know whose toes you are stepping on."

"I would like to contribute to the community . . . but which community?"

"A chamber music group for every other Tuesday? I don't think so."

"I left at 4:00 one Friday, and when I turned around to look back at the building from the parking lot he was watching me."

"I know he seems bright . . . but he is Jewish."

"I think Bill has a great future and his wife is just marvelous. Really beautiful."

"The middle management man must be able to tolerate a high degree of regimentation."

"I know this is difficult . . . I know you are working eighty hours a week . . . but, when you walk in here at 11:00 A.M. on Monday, it creates problems with the other people."

"It is serious . . . she got so bombed at the club on Saturday night they had to leave at 10:30."

"Don't complain to me about conformity. With the deferred income plan I have, I can't afford to think about it."

"The guy is really bright . . . but he comes out with the most outrageous ideas at times."

"Look, if you don't take our personality test, it's

okay, but, even at your high level, I am afraid this may blow your chances."

"It is smart, even during the most relaxed social occasions, to avoid deviation from generally accepted behavior."

"Sure, this company has an office caste system, and the truth is it helps to enforce a certain amount of deference to authority."

"We have found over the years that the well rounded man makes our best top management executive."

"If you have some Chinese style furniture you like . . . that's all right . . . but I don't think I would bring it into the office."

"You are young and you are new, but let me tell you what I think. If you are loyal to the company, the company will be loyal to you."

"We just don't hang pictures on the walls around here."

"The job description is a most important part of maintaining the interrelated functions within the structure of the organization."

"There is such a thing as a man being too lopsided . . . too much talent in one area and none at all in the others."

"Those men are monks . . . monks who traded their prayer books for a production line."

"There is no question that John is a good man . . . but it is also true that Betty has been a significant and positive force for him in the organization."

"Look around . . . you won't see anyone in this place more than five pounds overweight."

"To get to the top, a man has to put on a pair of blinders and shut out everything except business."

"A man may be judged, more than anything else, by whether, in countless large or small ways, he tells us he is loyal to the company."

"I have come to believe that it is easier to modify my needs than it is for the company to change its requirements."

"I like the way he talks, very deliberately, and the way he looks, slim, tall . . . impressive."

"It should be clear . . . you just don't smoke a big, black cigar in a full committee meeting like that."

"For God's sake, don't sit at that table . . . it's for senior vice presidents and above."

"You just don't get mink if the president's wife doesn't have mink."

How did all this get started? In earlier days, when many big companies were being formed, things were more rough-and-tumble. What was important then was productivity and effectiveness. You could pretty much do what you wanted to do if you got the job done. But in recent years we have seen big business change in many ways, and, in particular, *there has been strong emphasis on uniformity and conformity.* To what end? Knowingly or unknowingly, big business has adapted these concepts and these ideas from the military. For centuries, military people have known and recognized that by enforcing small rules and by obliterating individuality it is possible to produce optimum obedience. Big business needs more than obedience today. It needs excessive amounts of creative energy and drive in order to be able to fight increased levels of domestic and international competition. Unfortunately, some big companies will continue to perpetuate rules and regulations that produce conformity; but those that do should be certain they have technological superiority in the market place, or that their competition is not particularly strong or significant. They should be certain that they do not need to depend to a great degree on the talent and ingenuity and productivity and effort of the management people throughout the organization.

However, for those companies in a more competitive position who do need talent and creativity and believe their people are the most significant factors in success—for these companies a new view of this whole area of behavior within the organization is vitally important.

One way to change the face of a company in this connection is to put something in writing that clearly spells out what top management believes. Call it something like *A Declaration of Independence for the Individual in (Company Name)*. Once it is in writing, put it away for a couple of months. Then look at it again to see how it feels. If it is still right, then get it printed and post it throughout the company. Show it to everyone. Publicize it. Obviously, what goes into the declaration will vary by company, but here, in preliminary form, are two basic points, and some additional ideas, that should be included:

- You will have the opportunity to make maximum use of your talent and energy and productivity.
- You will be paid, so far as is humanly possible, in direct relationship to your productivity.

Suggested additional points:
- Make dress the province of the individual. Truly optional.
- Encourage full freedom of speech at all times and on all occasions.
- Above the clerical level, drop starting times, coffee breaks, lunch periods, and quitting times.
- Stop meddling in a man's life out of the office. What he does with his own time should be his business.
- Forget about his wife. Let her be as she is.
- Drop the use of personality and other such tests.
- Drop any rules in connection with office decoration.
- Above the clerical level, drop all job descriptions.
- Encourage effective participation in community affairs.
- Don't encourage nonconformity for its own sake, but don't discourage it either.

In general, communicate the basic idea that the personal wants and needs, both big and small, of the people who work in the company are very important and not secondary to those of the company.

You will have talent flocking to your company. You will have young, fresh, dynamic men and women attracted to the company. You will have taken a giant step in bridging the gap between today's college students and an older generation of businessmen—to the benefit of the company.

AREN'T YOU TIRED OF MOVING AROUND?

The practice of moving men and their families about the country and about the world had its beginning in the depression years of the thirties. In that era men would move almost any place and at any time to get a job or to hold a job. But in the first quarter of the century, corporate management people were not so mobile. What started in the thirties as an economic necessity became in the forties, fifties, and sixties a fundamental way of life in big business. This in part was caused by the phenomenal growth in individual companies and the resultant corporate need to get specific jobs done in specific areas. The "moving man" became part of big business, and with him the development of suburban communities that became the temporary homes of middle management and top executives in big business:

> Scarsdale, New York
> Greenwich, Connecticut

Birmingham, Michigan
Webster Groves, Missouri
Evanston, Illinois
Laguna Beach, California
Sandy Springs, Georgia

Real estate records show that in most of these and other similar suburban communities the number of moves in and out over a five-year period is equal to the total number of homes in the community. In other words, there is one hundred per cent turnover in homes occupied. The records of long distance movers show that as high as fifty per cent were made for clients in big business, i.e., they represented corporate personnel transferred from one area to another with the corporation paying the bill. Further evidence of this "moving man" characteristic is indicated in a study of big business leaders over the last twenty years. Corporation presidents, executive vice presidents, and vice presidents must be willing to move, and this has been a fundamental part of their progress and success. In fact, it is one of their few uniform characteristics. Companies have systemized the moving of people, developing special departments to aid the "moving man", which handle all of the housekeeping fuss of a move and pay for the bills. What is important, as far as the company is concerned and as far as the men who move are concerned, is the needs of the company.

After World War II men wanted security and

they found this in big business; but in exchange they had to be willing to move whenever and wherever the company decided. These men did not want to change the way big business operated or to challenge it or rebel against it. In the forties and fifties and sixties there was a general desire to join and to collaborate. Talk to any man who has moved and moved and you will find he has accepted the policies and philosophies that relate to his mobility, and rarely will there be a word of rebellion or a serious concern about the effects, on his family for instance. A man who accepts the philosophy of mobility has to put the considerations of his family in a secondary position. Every time he moves he has to disrupt the education of his children. Every time he moves he must leave friends. Every time he moves he goes from one "commuting suburb" to another. In these communities there are other men and other families who are also on the move. They become acquaintances quickly, if not close friends. In these communities there is no sense of belonging. There is no community life at all. It is up to the "local" people who were born and reared in the particular suburb—shopkeepers, real estate people, lawyers—to run the community and to be, in fact, the only participants in community life.

The growth of big business and the manpower requirements of big business demanded this mobility, and this mobility became a mandatory part of an individual's progress within the company. A man in big business who has turned down the next move, saying to the corporation, "There are things that are more important to me than the corporation's needs," has probably ruined his chances for further promotion. As a result, an ambitious individual automatically expects that he will move every three years or so. It is the belief of big business management that this mobility is one of its strengths. If the company has a serious problem in Dallas, it is possible, after a brief discussion and phone call or two, to put a man in Dallas who will correct that particular problem. Not only that, but the man can be there and operating within three or four days. Many times a man moves ahead of his family. He sets up his home in a motel room and goes to work in the new city on the new job. His family follows. Sometimes when the school year ends, sometimes at semester break. In the meantime, he commutes back to his family on weekends. For the corporation this is often productive. In fact, it is often so productive that it has become a hallmark of the key men in a company. They are the men who have moved, and will move, and move fast to get a job done.

Big business cannot adopt a policy which would not require a certain amount of mobility. However, big business should consider that to the talented people coming out of school today this practice of maximum mobility is particularly repugnant. The potential young executives of today have not gone through the depression of the thirties or World War II. They are better educated. They are well traveled. They are more sophisticated and often have different values than the men who lead big business today. Many of them are not willing to put their families second to the corporation. They are not willing to live in a "commuting" suburban community. They do want to join the social structure of the community in which they live and participate in it. They like the idea of having roots, and probably as important as anything else, they like the friends they have and want to continue to see them. Can big business fault them for these attitudes? Not at all. They are commendable expressions of human wants and needs that are important to the individual.

What should big business do? It is up to top management to begin now to change policies about mobility and use of manpower. An active effort should be made to avoid moving as often as in the past. Never? Probably not, but in some cases, even this is possible. Is such a program practical for a large company? I believe it is, if the company will actively work to solve its manpower needs by some other form of mobility. It isn't always necessary to move a person with a single discipline, such as selling, to fill this need in another geographical area. Big business can benefit by developing mobility between disciplines. Companies do not need to hold to the rigid lines of individual disciplines, since this is probably the major reason why there is so much mobility demanded. They can, instead, move people from one discipline to another to fill needs within the same geographical area, within the same plant, within the same operating unit. Smaller businesses do this all the time with good effect.

Big business should adopt as official policy that mobility is no longer a mandatory requirement for promotion. The individual should be able to reject a move and still find excellent opportunities for growth and promotion within the company. He should not find that his refusal to move his family or his refusal to leave his community and friends automatically puts an end to his progress.

It is possible for big business to develop a policy that will, once again, permit its best people and its most talented people to become whole people. Whole people, not only in terms of their talent and their work and their productivity for the company, but also in terms of their family, their friends, their community, and their life after retirement.

Florida and other such warm climate retirement states have become havens where retired business people herd together in compact groups. They retire to such places because after a career in big business they have nowhere else to go. Never having been part of a community, for over thirty years they have had only a shifting pattern of acquaintances and no long-term friends. They have moved five, six, perhaps eight times over the years. In fact, they have no place they consider home, and so they congregate in the warm places with others in the same condition. If you have ever visited one of these warm climate retirement villages, you will know just how sad it is.

MEMO 8

HUMAN MEASURE: WHAT MANAGEMENT LEFT OUT

The people in San Diego don't complain about size; but you hear such complaints from New Yorkers or the residents of L.A. For similar reasons people complain about General Motors and IBM and General Electric, and about big business in general. The solution is not to break up big business but to readjust its form of operation to bring it into scale with Human Measure.

What is Human Measure? Human Measure is knowing most of the places and streets and the neighborhoods in the city in which you live. Human Measure is knowing most of what's going on in the place where you work and in the work you do. Human Measure is knowing the people you work with. Human Measure is having just twenty-four hours to a day—so if someone takes three hours of his day just to commute to and from his job, he is using his time inhumanely. Human Measure is the smaller and medium size company, and the smaller and medium size city.

Columbia, Maryland lies halfway along the Washington/Baltimore corridor and has a population of ten thousand. Ultimately, it will have one hundred thousand residents and enough industry to be self-supporting. Columbia's developers started with a core city large enough to satisfy the needs of urban living, and then surrounded this core with separate villages of one thousand families each. Each of these villages is clustered around a group of shops and schools. Each of the villages has its own architectural style. Columbia, Maryland residents have developed pride in their villages and in the city itself, and this is not just because of the pretty streets, the abundance of greenery, the boating, the golf and tennis; the pride comes mainly from a sense of neighborhood and of neighborliness which the Human Measure of Columbia's plan permitted to flower.

Columbia's success in developing such a city is what we need more of today. What our survival demands is a new approach to living that will assert control over our industrial system and transform it in a way that makes life for the individual more productive by advancing his human values. It isn't necessary to destroy big business or to throw away our material wellbeing. It is necessary to guide big business into a new and better form, scaled in a variety of ways to Human Measure. To do this, big business is going to have to change many of its ways and in the process do away with many of its most dominant myths.

There is some talk of change in big business today but not much action. Most big companies are just building and building on top of the old organization structure. They are adding layers of vice presidents and overstructuring and getting extremely top-heavy. Take the title of "Executive Vice President". What does it mean? or "Senior Vice President"? Today business is getting title-happy. There are any number of companies where a sharp cut in the number of executives would produce a real improvement in efficiency.

Because of this proliferation of titles, the steps on the hierarchical structure are getting shorter and the names and identifications on the steps more elaborate. All the talk about democratic organization is pure rhetorical flourish to cover up the reality of dangerous overorganization.

The young people who join big business today are eager for challenging jobs. Instead, they are dropped into training programs and given fancy titles and fancy salaries and, finally, a file clerk's work. In theoretical knowledge, the young people today excel many of their elders. Some of them find themselves vice presidents at thirty but still working for some "old bookkeeper" who has been in the organization structure for thirty years or more. Too often young people today expect business to be run by what they have learned in school: by theory, by knowledge, by concepts, and by planning. Instead, they find big business run more by experience and expediency and by "who you know." Taking into account Human Measure is only one aspect of what must be a total reevaluation of the structure and methods of big business management, if the talents of these young people are not to go to waste.

FLATTENING THE "PYRAMID": THE FIRST GIANT STEP

Assume that you have just been appointed chief executive officer of a large business which has been operating for years with a typical hierarchical organization. A large staff organization oversees most of the communication between management and the operating divisions and it is through these staff people that top management decisions and actions are processed downward. It is also true that communication is sluggish and, at times, nonexistent. Missing is the intensity and drive that you, as the new chief executive officer, would like to see in the company.

What are you going to do about it? I suggest giving serious consideration to the establishment of a decentralized organization that includes a number of independent profit center units. How to make it work? I suggest the following steps:

1. Commit yourself completely to decentralization. You have to believe it will work

and you have to believe that it is the absolutely right thing to do for your company.

2. You must personally evaluate all the key people in your company. You have to select those who are capable of running decentralized profit centers. You will find them both within the current operating units and the staff organization. In fact, these will be the fifteen best people in the company. So far there isn't anything very revolutionary about all this except that *you are going to have to let them go*. It is probable that you have been running a big organization previously, and you are used to the power and authority that are part of the hierarchical organization. But if you want to revitalize the company, you will have to relinquish much of it.

3. Once the people are in place and the profit centers established, you will instruct them to develop their operating plans for the year ahead (or two or three years). The extent of the plan depends upon the industry and the company. This plan will include proposed sales, cost of product, operating expenses, and profit objective for the particular year. It should not be a "sales objective plan," with wishful thoughts about what can possibly be achieved if everything works right. This has to be a hard-nosed plan, and the operating head of this business must know that what you look to him for is that profit figure.

Part of the plan for the year should also be the definition of the specific projects that are going to be put in place to achieve additional growth over and above the plan. These can be new products or new forms of distribution, new advertising and promotion plans, new sales plans, personnel changes, etc.

4. There should be a formal presentation of the plan to you by the management of the operating profit center which must result in agreement that the plan is right.

5. Let them go. Let your operating people have the full authority to make decisions and take action within the plan; this involves decisions about people, about products, about production, everything. They do not need to get approval on operating decisions, and you do not need to check up on every action. They are free to do what they think is required to achieve the proposed goals.

6. To keep some form of control, your treasurer or controller has to have a direct line to the treasurer or controller of each profit center. He does not need to work through the operating unit head. Instead, the two financial people can exchange information directly. (This part of the plan must be clearly understood by everyone concerned.) The reason for this should be obvious. In a decentralized profit center operation such as this, there has to be some check-and-balance mechanism, aside from your own direct contact with the chief operating officer of the profit center. It gives you another view of the operation, aside from the one you receive from the chief operat-

ing officer. It gives you a cold and objective "numbers" view of how things are going, while at the same time permitting your profit center operating head to function freely within the plan. But—to emphasize again—in the area of operations, there can be no interference. There must be, at the profit center level, full authority to make the operational decisions necessary to execute the plan.

7. You should have a monthly face-to-face meeting in which a report is made on how the profit center is doing in sales and profit against the previous year's performance and against the operating budget. At this meeting your profit center chief can bring in as many people as he wants from his side of the operation. You should have yourself and your controller and not many more people involved.

About this time it should be clear to you that you are operating without a large staff. You don't need it. You have committed much of your authority and responsibility to the operators of the profit center. You have a one-to-one relationship with these operating heads, and that's as it should be. All you need to do to destroy that relationship is insert a couple of layers of staff people in between you and the line, and you're on your way back to the old hierarchical structure that was in place before you took over. Staff people can kill profit center operators.

8. Keep the paper flow to a minimum. Reserve most of your communication for your

monthly face-to-face meetings with the profit center head and his controller. Don't have a lot of memoranda and reports flowing back and forth. Make these face-to-face meetings action oriented. When the profit center operator needs a decision that's above and beyond his plan, make it at the meeting, or make it at the next meeting.

More and more we see companies turning to decentralized profit centers as a form of management. One major company in the brewing industry recently converted their regional sales offices into eight regional profit centers with separate presidents responsible for profit as well as building sales and controlling costs. Each president has a separate profit sharing plan and an incentive program for his operating unit. The company has taken this route because it found that it was impractical to apply programs on a national basis. What was right for the Southeast was not necessarily right for the Midwest, and what was right for the Midwest didn't work at all in the Northeast. The company consequently divided the country into eight natural regions, making sure that *within each region* the marketing situation for the company's products was generally uniform. The eight best marketing men in the company were put in place as presidents to run each of these eight operations. The marketing plans for each company varied considerably in the first year of planning. The eight plans were developed at the local level by the president and his people and then presented at company headquarters for approval. Each of these eight plans included specifics on product emphasis, distribution, promotion, advertising, publicity, and selling. Each of these plans presented a complete operating statement, including sales, cost of sales, operating expenses, and profit. Each of these plans became the guide for the year ahead.

Many companies are large enough now to have this type of regional profit center decentralization. Effective central control has become increasingly difficult. Most companies can be more productive if they are oriented to the considerable differences in the geographical regions of the country. Regional tastes and regional wants and needs vary to a considerable degree. Climate is a major factor in determining this. Some of the gasoline companies have recognized this by changing gasolines to fit the various climate demands.

But more important, decentralized profit centers will get more people into the decision-making function and closer to the action. They will know, on a firsthand and personal basis, what is needed to get results.

With such a decentralized profit center operation, there will develop within the organization a drive and a lift and an initiative that are impossible to find in the typical hierarchical organization. When good people are given authority and responsibility for a plan, they can and will work harder, more imaginatively, and more effectively than under any other circumstances. If you have picked the right people to head up your profit centers, your life is going to be easier, your job less wearing, and the profit of the total corporation is bound to grow.

MEMO 10

EVERY MAN FOR HIMSELF
—FOR THE GOOD
OF THE COMPANY

The entrepreneurial spirit is not dead. Within big business the spark and drive can be ignited, given the proper environment. But this environment can only be created when the individual's goals are integrated with the goals of the company. There is in almost every person the desire for self-achievement and self-fulfillment that originally motivated the entrepreneur in the early years of business in this country. Just think what can happen to the big business that develops a new attitude to stimulate this "entrepreneurial spirit" on the part of hundreds of individuals within the company.

In the old hierarchical organization structure, the company just simply tells the person what his job is and how to do it. The company establishes its goals and tells the person to reach these goals. The company then evaluates the person's performance and tells him whether or not he has done a good job.

Finally, the company either rewards him or doesn't reward him.

However, more effective leadership of people is achieved when the goals of the individual are related to and integrated with the goals of the company. Or, to put it another way, the goals of the company cannot be established and then merely presented to the individual because then these goals will never become his goals, too. The goals of the individual have to be considered before the goals of the company are finalized, and the goals of the company have to be considered before the goals of the individual are finalized. Obviously, this is not a straight-line process, and there is an integration and exchange of ideas that is fundamental. There has to be excellent communication between the company and the individual. Once goals for the company and the individual are integrated, then the individual will provide the self-control and self-direction needed to achieve these goals.

What are the methods which will create this new attitude? *The key management premise should be participation.* A person gets to participate in all of the significant decisions that relate to his career within the company.

Step 1—Defining the job. The first area of participation for an individual and for the company is in defining what is his job. The individual is asked to list what he thinks should be his major responsibilities as well as his minor responsibilities. He is not given a written job description and told to work within its strictures. Written job descriptions are exercises in bureaucratic futility. It is impossible to create written job descriptions that are effective because the way a job is done must vary with the individual. So the man helps define his job as he sees it, and then the company does exactly the same thing. Ideas are exchanged, and finally, together, the individual and the company settle on the definition of the job he is to do. In this process the individual feels that he must not automatically accept what the company or his manager says. The company's job is to help him and to come up with a job description that satisfies both the individual and the company; but the company can't help if the individual simply defers to the company, if he accepts the old attitudes and feels that the best thing for him to do is to do what he is told. The individual must look on the company as a collaborator whose experience and knowledge are at his disposal, with the understanding that there will be differences, but that these differences can be resolved by effective communication.

Big business has the obligation of conveying this premise to the people who work in big business. This isn't something that can be sent out in an internal memorandum with any good effect. It is achieved largely through frank and honest discussions in which the company representative impresses on the individual his desire to put all his knowledge and experience at the individual's disposal.

When this happens, a dramatic change can take place in the individual's perception of himself and his job.

Business must adopt the attitude that the employee has the major responsibility for his own development, but also that the company can help in this development. The company should conceive of integration as an active process which inevitably resolves differences of opinion and argument. The company knows that the establishment of this kind of relationship takes time, but that its long-term results will be well worth the effort. There is a clear understanding that as the person grows the job will grow and the job definition will be subject to change in contrast to the out-of-date concept of the organization as a series of pre-determined slots into which individuals are placed.

Step 2—Setting objectives. Again, the premise should be participation. The employee isn't simply given objectives by the company but, instead, contributes his own thinking as to what the objectives or targets should be for himself and for his function as a whole. At the same time he must ask himself what steps he is going to take to achieve these objectives. In short, the company says to the person: "We don't want to tell you how to do your job, but we would like you to do some careful thinking about how you are going to proceed. When you get this thinking done, then we ought to get together and discuss your ideas."

In contrast, in the conventional process

objectives are conceived at higher levels and imposed on lower levels of the organization, because only the higher levels have available the broad knowledge necessary for planning. To some extent, this is always going to be true, but there is an important difference between the kind of planning in which a central group determines in detail what each division or department or person will do and that in which the central group communicates what it believes to be desirable overall objectives of the company and then asks each individual unit to determine what it can contribute.

The acceptance of responsibility for self-direction and self-control by the individual employee is correlated with the commitment to objectives. Genuine commitment is seldom achieved when objectives are handed down from above. Passive acceptance is more likely, or even indifference or resistance. But, when there is some degree of mutual involvement in the determining of objectives, then the results achieved can be far more impressive.

To be sure, some people will set unrealistic goals, particularly the first time they are given the opportunity. *Experience has indicated that the usual problem is that the goals are set too high and not too low.* While the company can, through judicious advice, help the individual adjust unrealistic goals, there may often be greater long-range advantages in permitting him to learn by experience rather than simply telling him where his planning is unrealistic or inadequate.

74

Step 3—Doing the job. Here the aim should be to develop the individual and produce further growth in his competence by his full acceptance of responsibility. In short, if a person has had the chance to participate in the definition of his job and in the setting of goals for himself, then all that can be done to create the proper environment for his self-motivation and self-direction has been achieved. Now the company must let him go. Now the company must treat him as though he were an independent entrepreneur. Now the company must let him provide his own stimulation and drive in attacking the job and achieving the objectives.

If everything else is going reasonably well, the company shouldn't harass him about mistakes. There isn't anyone who can do every job perfectly, and a good average is to do more things right than wrong. Pick your own level: sixty–forty; seventy–thirty; or eighty–twenty. If big business can accept the possibility that mistakes will be made, it is going to be more than compensated for by the increased creative effort applied by the individual in reaching the mutual objectives of himself and the company.

Step 4—Appraisal of results. Instead of having the company evaluate and appraise what has been achieved, the company asks the individual to do it. The company asks the person how he evaluates what he has accomplished with reference to the objectives which he set earlier. In the process, the individual can develop his next goal and work pattern for the ensuing period.

In short, the typical personnel appraisal, practiced for years and in almost all big businesses in which superiors rate subordinates, is out of date. The employee rates himself and *then* reports to management.

Step 5—Salary adjustment. This leads me to one of the most difficult areas for big business to change: salary administration. Traditionally, if a person did a good job, he was given an increase in salary as a reward. We know now that money alone doesn't provide adequate motivation. Not that economic reward is no longer important, but money doled out in increments over a period of time in response to achievements will not make people more productive. In the proposed open-minded attitude of big business toward its employee, salary levels would be established more by the "going rate" within the industry than by a superior's decision. In short, even in this delicate area a good person who is doing a good job and knows it can, in part, "participate" with his company in establishing his proper salary level.

The same procedure may be applied to promotion. The company and the person together decide what path he is going to travel and what are his next objectives as far as job-to-job levels are concerned. (Incidentally, this does at some point permit the person to say to the company that he doesn't want to move, that he likes his life and his community and his job and doesn't want to change.)

Perhaps the biggest change required in current practices with respect to promotion and placement of people has to do with the relation of the individual himself to this process. All too often he tends to be a pawn in the organization chessboard. Plans are made with respect to his career which may have profound effects upon his most important goals and needs. Yet he is likely to have no voice in these plans and to remain in complete ignorance of them until after the decision has been reached. Moreover, the company's needs are given priority, almost without consideration, over his needs. If his goals and needs are considered at all, it is likely to be in the paternalistic sense of deciding "what is good for him".

Big business has to stop acting like a policeman or a stern grandfather. It has to recognize that once the company and the individual have defined the job and have set the goals, it must let him go. Let him do the job, achieve the goals, and make the mistakes. Let him realize the economic rewards and the rewards of self-esteem, recognition, and self-fulfillment. In this environment the individual will have an opportunity to fully realize his potential; he will have an opportunity to produce to the best of his ability and to fully utilize his talents and capabilities.

No longer will an employee grumble at the end of his career, "All I got was a gold watch after thirty-five years". Instead, he will be genuinely grateful to the company for giving him an opportunity for self-fulfillment—the greatest possible reward for a lifetime of work.

MEMO 11

PROFIT-SHARING:
IT PAYS ITS OWN WAY

Profit sharing has long been part of many big business remuneration plans. Usually profit sharing is based on an established percent of before-tax profit. Characteristically, these plans are attractive to employees when they consider the "total package" that they receive from the company. This includes of course salary, insurance, paid vacations, retirement plans, and profit sharing. These profit sharing plans usually do not specifically relate to an individual's performance as much as to his salary level and longevity. Typically, these plans reflect the company's total performance. Such profit sharing plans in time become somewhat invisible. They are taken for granted, and it is easy to see why because, in fact, people may receive a share of profit when they have made no specific, measurable contribution to the profit. (Often, the profit for a particular period is determined by industry conditions and the general economic situation in the country.)

I recommend something new and different. It is *a Profit Gain Incentive Plan*. This plan gives reward in direct response to a performance that contributes directly to profit. It is in direct contrast to the old hierarchical pat-on-the-head and reward-from-above approach. With this plan a person works and contributes and earns his own reward. It is not just "given to him". More people have an opportunity to become partners with management in contributing to the profit growth of the company, and this partnership helps to generate the ideas and energies that contribute importantly to the growth of the business.

In this plan the amount of remuneration is tied to performance in one of two areas: (1) reducing costs, and (2) building sales. The emphasis and reward paid for a profit gain contribution in either of these two areas will vary of course, since some companies are sales-oriented while others are primarily production-oriented.

The Profit Gain Incentive Plan gives every participating member of the organization an opportunity to contribute his brains and physical effort to the improvement of the profit of a company. It lets a person way down the line in production make a contribution and receive a reward. It creates an environment stimulating to everyone. Consequently, it generates more energy, more enthusiasm, and more productivity from individuals within the company. As employees become more aware of productivity and their opportunity to share in the profit gains, they will turn to the people not contributing and ask questions. "Why is he allowed to keep his position if he is not contributing? Are we obligated to cut him in on the profit gains that we produce?"

At any level down to the smallest group, the starting point for a program directed at reducing costs and increasing productivity must be an expenditure figure for a particular year which is used as the norm. It could be the dollars paid for manpower in relation to the product produced, or a cost percent of total revenues. What is important is that a fair base figure is established and that the people who are going to work for profit gain incentives know exactly what the base is and how it has been determined.

Some flexibility is needed to take into account product mix, inventory, work in process, and the market situation. But what you are saying to the people is simply this: "If you will figure out a way to produce more for less or to produce more at the same expense, the company is going to achieve a certain profit gain and we are going to share this profit gain with you."

The second major area for profit gains obviously comes from sales growth, and here programs are easier to establish. In addition to ordinary profit sharing programs, many sales forces already have bonus programs that are based upon sales gains.

The base figure could be the previous year's sales by product, or the budget figure for the year. In any case, the salesman knows ahead of time precisely what is to be his sales base. In the ordinary plan, a bonus is paid on the basis of sales increase. In my proposed plan, the salesman is paid on *the profit gain* achieved as the result of the sales gain. In the process, the salesman becomes a participant in helping to contribute to the economic success of the company. He is not just a man who sells and lets management take care of that other consideration called profit. He understands that he is a contributor to profit gains in a very real way because he gets to share in them.

This can occur in two ways. For each product there is a sales volume level that produces a normal or acceptable level of profit. Sales above this level increase the profit margin per item up to the level of optimum efficiency and optimum profit. As he makes more sales that produce larger increments of profit, the salesman is given a larger and larger percentage of that increase in profits as his reward.

A second method of relating the salesman's rewards to profit gain involves those products that are more profitable than others. According to the company and the nature of the products, the second method may be used in the same company concurrently with the first or it may not. For sales of these products with higher profit margins per item, the salesman earns a larger percentage of the profit gains as his reward. He receives a "normal" reward for sales of products with normal or average profit. He receives less than normal reward for sales of products with smaller profit margins per item.

In a vitamin and health supplement company, for example, ten per cent commission is given on the vitamin line, while only five per cent is given on a group of private label items, to insure maximum effort in selling the company line, which has a higher profit margin.

In general, how much of the profit gains should be shared with the contributors? This will vary with each company, and it will vary within departments, and it will vary by function, and it will vary down to the very last person who gets to share in the profit gain as the result of making a contribution to it. But keep in mind one of the basic premises that we have already established: that you are, in a tangible sense, making the people who contribute to the profit gain your *partners*. You are asking them to use their brains and their energies to work with you to create profit gains. It is important that when giving rewards these new management attitudes are honored and not all of the cream goes to the top. The profit gain sharing can be as little as five per cent, though it should rarely be this small. It might be ten per cent, or even more, of the before-tax profit gain. In fact, on a purely theoretical basis, some people believe that the profit gain share level should be fifty per cent—half for the producers and half for the stockholders. I have seen plans that have been extremely productive at the ten per cent level and, at the other extreme, I knew of a company which used a fifty per cent plan. This company was undergoing a reorganization in production and it was believed that a gain in productivity was mandatory in a particular year. It was understood by all concerned that this fifty per cent plan would be reduced in subsequent years. Management knew that the immediate productivity gains and the resultant profit gains would have a lasting effect on the success of the company. In short, be bold in your profit gain sharing because the long-term results can and will be startling.

Such a program, when properly initiated, quickly gains genuine acceptance and provides real motivation. It is a means of promoting collaboration within the company and within groups. Petty competition for job promotion tends to decline.

With the Profit Gain Incentive Plan, employees are able to trace directly the results of various changes and innovations stimulated by their efforts and to see the connection between what they do and what the organization achieves. The result for the employees is a very real and quite sophisticated understanding of the profitability of the company gained by direct experience.

MEMO 12

HOME OFFICE STAFF:
A LUXURY
NO COMPANY CAN AFFORD

Before business became big business, almost all of the key people in a company were likely to be "line" people. Initially, these were sales people, or production people, or finance people. As business grew, the disciplines expanded and subdivided. Under a hierarchical organization structure, top management developed the staff function and staff organization as a means of maintaining power and control. The hierarchical-style manager has found that, even though a big business is complex, there is a way out of his dilemma. He can delegate and yet keep control, by assigning to people on his staff some of his responsibility for supervising the work of line people. The staff has made it possible for the hierarchical-style manager to make all the essential decisions and then let the specialists, or line people, "work out the details." After he has set a policy and, perhaps, specific goals, then he has his staff follow through and check up and coordinate the implementation.

This practice conflicts with the kind of leadership big business must furnish in the nineteen seventies and beyond. The new leader in big business has to be prepared to relinquish, not delegate, a large amount of control, which he is able to do because he has confidence in the willingness and ability of his line people to achieve the organization's objectives. He also recognizes that he must risk some poor judgments and even mistakes on their part in order to permit them an adequate degree of autonomy to function at their best.

Typically, a staff person is personally prepossessing and gets on well with top management people. His education has focused on his particular specialty, whether finance or engineering or business management. He has been taught to seek and find "the best answer." Because he is well educated, he usually has great confidence in the objectivity of his approach to problems. He expects the resultant solutions to be immediately and gratefully accepted by the organization. Management by direction and control seems perfectly reasonable to him.

However, the staff person often finds that many of his fellow workers on the line are not reasonable human beings. Not only are they less than properly impressed by him as a person, they frequently reject the results of his studies or refuse to use his "latest-model" techniques. The staff person is likely to put great store in standardization and well worked out procedures and rules. The coordinative function is his meat. Here is a way to minimize personal, subjective, and unpredictable elements in human behavior and to obtain a kind of direction and control which will really improve the effectiveness of the enterprise.

In too many big businesses today, the staff people are in control. The central chain of command from top management to line is becoming increasingly dependent on specialized staff groups; and the staff groups, which were originally put in place as advisory and service groups without authority, are becoming, by virtue of the importance of their knowledge and skill and because of management's delegation to them of control and coordinative functions, the dominant, influential core of the organization. In one very large conglomerate, seventy per cent of the personnel above the second level of supervision are staff, and the proportion is growing.

This is not to suggest that the staff people do not have a proper place within big business. Staff people can serve the organization well in many fields, which include public relations, legal counsel, government relations, and the like.

But the spirit and the drive and the innovative capacity of big business are being hurt by the growth of the staff function when the staff function includes the control plus responsibility functions. Big business must change its attitude about leadership, and part of that change in attitude requires that big business return to line control, line authority, and line responsibility. Line people must set their own goals; they must be given the opportunity to work to achieve these goals in their own way; and then they must evaluate and report on their performance exactly as individuals should do throughout the corporation.

Too long have the staff people within big business been acting as policemen through the use of delegated management authority. This hasn't happened suddenly, as we have noted. Staff people evolved into positions of control. When staff people are given the right to gather detailed information about a particular division or function that includes information on the performance of all of the subordinates in the division, they invariably usurp from the division manager a certain degree of his authority and control. They are also in the home office, close to top management. Staff people see top management frequently; typically, daily. A transfer of power and authority is produced by osmosis. Slowly but surely, the staff person begins to believe that he has all the power of top management. He begins to assume more and more power and finally brings to his relationship with line people an attitude of absolute authority.

But this same staff person who wields authority and control is not responsible, in the final analysis, for results. In a big business a debilitating condition results. The staff person, in many cases, sets goals for the line person. The line person is told what to do and how to do it. The staff person controls the information on performance. Then, when the line person doesn't achieve the goals or do the job the way he has been directed, the staff person is in a position to report to top management on his performance, or lack of performance.

Line people must be given the opportunity to establish their own goals and to be in a position of self-control. When they can operate with this degree of autonomy and indedependence, an environment of self-fulfillment is created that, in turn, produces the drive, enthusiasm, and imagination that will get the job done.

What is the appropriate role for staff people? For one, staff people can make a significant contribution in strategy planning for the company. They can develop specialized knowledge and information to help management in its long-range planning. Often the research and knowledge of a staff group will be the major determinant of organization policy or management strategy. The role of the staff person in providing such help may be compared to the role of an architect, working with a client on a new home. The client has ideas about the kind of house he wants, and he has lots of experience in living. The architect has professional knowledge that can help the client end up with a house that will better serve his needs than one which the client might design all by himself. The problem faced by the architect is to bring about an integration of his professional knowledge and the client's own ideas in such a way that the client will be satisfied with the result. Staff people can, and do, make a significant contribution in big business by providing the specialized information input that is necessary for the development of long-range strategies and plans for the company. But for the same reason that an unbridled architect will often design a home that is unsuitable for his client, staff people must not be allowed to usurp the functions of top management.

Staff people can also be helpful in special problem solving as long as they realize their limits. Very often, once they get into specific problems, they forget themselves and, in a sense, take over a line operation. Field visits of headquarter's staff people are often devoted almost exclusively to selling programs for headquarters-designed programs, or on checking up to see whether the field is using them effectively. Nevertheless, there are special problems that develop in the typical big business that do require the use of staff people for their solution. For these restricted purposes staff people serve line people by enabling them to continue to devote their full attention to their own functions and goals.

But staff people should never report on the organization and on the performance of line people. Line people must do their own reporting and their own analyses of performance and make these reports personally to top management if the new attitudes toward work are to last. If staff people report to management on the performance of line people, then the staff people inevitably assume positions above the line people. Big business must never again permit the staff function to dominate. Big business has to keep the staff function in a secondary position of service to management and service to the line.

What should big business do about the large staffs that have developed over the years? A big business that continues to function under the hierarchical structure shouldn't do a thing. The large staff is absolutely necessary to maintain the top of the pyramid in place. But if a big business does accept the new leadership attitudes, then it is clear that major changes should be made in the staff function.

This should not be any halfway measure. In some cases, the entire staff function should be dropped. In some cases, a few functions should be maintained. (Keep in mind that the staff function has to be tightly controlled or it will blossom forth again.) In most cases, no staff at all is the best policy of all. The best of the staff people can be sent to the line, and the others can become independent consultants to companies that don't know any better.

In the beginning, the line came first, and now, once again, the line must come first.

MEMO 13

THE "GENERALIST" HOAX

The complexity of big business has fostered a new breed of executive, the generalist. But before business became big business it was, of course, much simpler, and the functions of production and selling and bookkeeping (finance) represented the three basic disciplines required for the operation of a business. As businesses grew bigger and bigger, these three basic disciplines subdivided and produced new disciplines that were more precise and narrower in range. The broad discipline of selling became a series of disciplines, including selling, customer service, product service, distribution, advertising, promotion, market research, packaging. Production also became product design and testing. Bookkeeping evolved into the broader discipline of finance with many sub-disciplines, including cost control, stockholder relations, equity financing, etc. The interaction between these new disciplines and the three fundamental disciplines of production, selling, and bookkeeping has become more and more complex.

It is more difficult to communicate effectively in big business, more difficult to get people to understand what must be done, and more difficult to motivate them accordingly.

This condition has fostered the generalist who knows a little bit about many disciplines, but does not have to have in-depth knowledge in any one discipline. The argument goes that big business is so complex, with so many disciplines involved, that the generalist is *the new manager type.*

Typically, the generalist likes being "above" the workaday disciplines. He often prides himself on being a good administrator.

But there is a basic flaw and a truly serious problem in the generalist philosophy of management. The generalist doesn't get too deeply into anything in the business. Instead, he brings to specific problems and specific situations the attitude of the consultant. He may be bright, and he may have good judgment. But the generalist believes that his job is merely to point the way, and he doesn't believe that he has the responsibility to actually do the job or contribute to the job himself. *In short, he does not accept the philosophy of leadership in which co-contribution is mandatory.* He is a believer in the hierarchical philosophy of management. He believes that the command tent should be well behind the lines and far from the fighting. He believes in much of the mystique of the hierarchy. The symbols of management are very important to him: the size and position of his office, for example.

The generalist stays away from specific involvement and it is rare that you will find him fully committed to a project or a program. He is interested in the result, of course, but not in contributing to the work required to achieve that result. The generalist rarely goes out on the limb. He doesn't like to have specific responsibility assigned to him within a particular discipline. The generalist prides himself on the fact that he does not possess skills in a particular discipline, and, when you talk to enough generalists, you will find that their real belief is that working within any of the specific disciplines of big business is beneath them. You will not find generalists who sell, or design, or produce, or publicize; they merely administrate.

In contrast, what happens when a person who knows a particular discipline evolves into a leadership role in big business? One man I know started out as an accountant. He was a brilliant accountant, and he became a brilliant manager. But his work as an accountant and his training as an accountant automatically insured his belief in a management philosophy of the co-contributor.

Many presidents I know were originally salesmen, and they worked their way up through the organization from field sales jobs. Naturally, this is good experience. But more important, such men worked as co-contributors. Once a person works in a discipline and produces results in a discipline, he will find it extremely difficult to forget what he has learned. In some cases he may carry the discipline (selling or research or accounting), into higher and higher levels of management and always maintain a particular bias in this regard. This may produce, in some cases, a somewhat lopsided attitude as far as the way the business is run and how he approaches his job. Obviously, if he cannot in part divorce himself from his discipline, he will limit how far he can move within an organization. But the important thing is that the person who has such a discipline carries with him to higher levels of management *an attitude of work, co-contributing, and leadership that is invaluable to big business.* Big business was once led only by men who came up through the ranks from particular disciplines, and it is only in the period since 1946 that the generalist has evolved and become a significant factor in big business.

Business schools have contributed to the generalist theory, and big business has gone for it. Immediately after World War II many businesses brought military men into high levels of management. The military men came in totally steeped in the hierarchical philosophy of organization and also with the conviction that as generalists and as men of judgment, character, and integrity, they could make a significant contribution to big business. There were some exceptions, but, as a rule, most of these military men were not effective managers in big business.

Big business should rid itself of the generalist theory of management. It doesn't need generalists even if there is a complexity of disciplines required to run big business. Instead big business needs more men who are real leaders, who come from specific disciplines, who know how to produce and how to get results themselves, and who have a basic philosophy of management that is based on being co-contributors with the people they lead.

MEMO 14

HOW TO PRUNE EXECUTIVE DEADWOOD

I must tell you at the start that this is one of those *Rah Rah* memos. It is a lot easier to see what ought to be done than to actually get it done.

Almost every big company has some executive deadwood around. It is the natural result of great size and of a complex organization. It is also the result in many large companies of frequent changes in top management.

When men grow old or tired or lose their drive or have been promoted beyond their natural abilities, some people believe they should merely be "cut out" in order to preserve the strength of the organization. There are companies that are indeed so ruthless. But typically, these companies are terrible places to work. They have high executive turnover. The skills and talents of their people are effective only for short runs. The men in these companies have "flash" careers. In the long run these companies don't attract top quality talent and can't hold on to men of real ability.

But too many big businesses work the other side of the street and don't do anything at all about the deadwood at executive levels. All too many of them believe that this is something they have to live with in a large organization.

Unfortunately, many of the men at executive levels who are no longer productive are very loyal to the corporation. They are cooperative and willing, if not effective. Many are great memo-writers and meeting-attenders. They quickly agree with whatever a superior says. They often do quite a bit of politicking to maintain their positions.

The problem with such men is not only that they are not productive, but that they reduce the drive and spirit and effectiveness of the men in the company who do have talent and do get things done.

The solution is *not* to handle each and every such situation on an individual basis. Individual handling often means a company fails to cut out its deadwood. The problem is perpetuated, and the solution merely put off.

Instead I recommend that the board of directors and the chief executive officer initiate a formal program of *early, early retirement.* Obviously, there isn't a problem of executive deadwood among men who are in their middle thirties or forties. The problems occur with men beyond these age groups. The company should therefore establish an early, early retirement plan that begins at fifty and runs at ascending levels of retirement pay on a year-by-year basis through sixty. This early, early retirement plan should be in writing and known to all executives. The retirement remuneration would run from the date of retirement to death and would be established at a percentage of salary depending on the age of the man. What this percentage of salary is at fifty or fifty-five or sixty is something that will vary by company. It may start as low as ten per cent or go up to as high as fifty per cent. Each plan will have to be scaled down from the regular retirement plan of the company (at age sixty-five or sixty or whatever is the current age for retirement).

This plan might seem expensive, but, in fact, it will not be so. The money spent on early retirements to cut out executive deadwood is money that is being invested in support of the best and most productive people in the company.

Besides, when a man is no longer productive and no longer as effective as he should be, in most cases he has a sense of this. He may do a lot of things to hang on and protect himself, but often he knows that he is not doing all that he should do, or is not capable of doing all that he ought to do. This is the hard truth. Men who are tired or who have lost their drive or who have been promoted beyond their natural ability sometimes will be surprised when this is told to them, but often, in time, they will come to accept the truth.

When you look at these executives closely, you can see that they are protective, defensive, negative, unenergetic, and untalented; and if you take these same words and use them to describe a company, you will find a company that is standing still, a company that is not aggressively growing, a company that is not highly profitable, a company that is not strongly competitive.

A company cannot accept the notion that its size means a lot of deadwood around won't make much difference because these nonproductive men are easily absorbed into the organization structure. Nonproductive people poison the environment and produce a strong negative influence. It is clear to a carpenter that he can't build a piece of furniture around a piece of deadwood, and a company can't build a strong organization structure around executive deadwood.

Once in a while it is possible to move such executives to new and different disciplines. Sometimes it is possible to move them over and down to different jobs, get them out of the way and, hopefully in the process, get some productivity for the expense involved. This works once in a while, but most of the time it does not do much for the man who is moved, or for the company either. It has a souring effect on all concerned.

The intelligent solution is to face the problem squarely and get the board to establish a plan of early, early retirement; then go to work and effect it for those people who no longer are productive. Or, as the president of the company, if you don't want to do this, the *least* you can do is accept early retirement for yourself.

MEMO 15

TEAMWORK AT THE TOP

If you and your executive committee are working productively as a team, you should all get approximately the same base salary.

Look at it this way. At the very top of the old-fashioned hierarchical ladder, there is a tremendous jump in salary level. The president's salary and bonus can exceed $200,000, while most of the division managers may get something well under $70,000. In company after company the top man's salary is often double that of the second man and triple that of the other top executives. Traditionally, in big business the climb is steep, the path often tortuous, and the final reward tremendous.

Why? Are the people who eventually get these tremendous salaries at the very top of big business really that much better? Do they actually make such a difference in the progress and profitability and the growth of the companies that they head? There are always exceptions, of course, but the truth is that in most cases their contributions are not all that significant. It is rare that one man makes a great difference in the way big business performs today.

This step-up salary structure is a direct result of the vertical structure of big business. There are ladders to climb; there are people to beat out; and the fight is never-ending. After all this fighting and scratching and climbing, there has to be a reward, and that reward comes in the form of a big salary jump. Even on a monetary basis, these top salaries don't really mean all that much: taxes take most of it away. But tremendous salaries are a point of honor furnishing tangible recognition that a man has made it all the way. They are not paid because the man is that much better than his top level co-workers or because he does that much more for the company. These salaries are paid because of a hierarchical organization structure that demands this kind of recognition.

Such an organizational structure and resultant attitude will not serve big business well in the future. There should not be a tremendous gap in the salaries of the top executives of big business because when such considerations as seniority, big business politics, and other accidental factors are removed, frequently a dozen or more men in a big business can step into the chief executive officer's position and run the company effectively. At General

Motors there must be twenty men who are capable, right at this moment, of running the company. At Goodyear there are at least a half dozen men who can walk down that long hall with the oak panels, slip into the chief executive's chair and run the company just about the way it has been run right along.

The size, complexity, and momentum of a big business are such that today no one person makes a really big difference. It is impossible for anyone to step into the chief executive's position and actually change the course, progress, and form of a company in the period in which he functions. The variety of disciplines, including finance, production, engineering, sales, marketing, plus the sub-breakdowns within divisions, means many, many people contribute to the success of a big business. But big business needs a stronger creative effort from more people at the top. Big business needs better teamwork from more people at the top. Big business needs less of the internal politicking and in-fighting that characterize the conditions of all too many companies. Too much energy is wasted fighting inside competition and not enough attention is given to fighting outside competition. Too many actions are designed to further careers within the company rather than to further the company. Too many memorandums are written to impress people in the hierarchical structure rather than to get more business or to produce more profit.

This is not to suggest that a big company doesn't need a person at the top who makes the final decisions. Every big business needs a leader, just as any organization needs a leader; but the leader in big business needs with him a group of co-leaders, and this fact can best be recognized and impressed upon the organization by giving all of these co-leaders just about the same salary as the chief executive.

It makes sense to have each member of the executive committee representing the various disciplines in the company earn about the same salary, give or take five thousand. These people would then become equal partners in building the company. Should a production manager earn as much money as a marketing director? The production manager doesn't look as distinguished as the marketing director; he doesn't speak as well as the marketing director. But the marketing director can't do the production manager's job; and the production manager can, in his own way, with efficiency in production, make a contribution to profit that is the equivalent of whatever sales growth is achieved by the marketing director. Should a financial manager receive just about the same salary as the chief executive officer? I believe he should, because he can, with sophisticated cost control programs and sophisticated use of capital, make a contribution to the growth and profit of the business that is uniquely his and that comes only from his particular talent and discipline. It is certain that in this executive committee the personalities will not all be equal. Some will be more impressive than others. Some will be more articulate and more effective in the meetings than others. But each of these people, in his own particular discipline, will have an opportunity to contribute to the growth and profit of the company, which could be appropriately recognized by an (almost) equal salary structure.

In the executive committee the odds are that the committee members themselves, over a period of time, will recognize without much question who the successor should be for the chief executive's position. If there are two people who are right for the job, as is often the case, so be it. The point is there is no need to have the company lose one of these people in a life-or-death struggle for the top spot and the prestige step-up in salary. If they are both earning about the same salary and that doesn't change, this is tangible evidence of the equality of their worth to the company.

Some years ago, a man I knew became president of a big food company. His top competititor in the firm was running one of the most successful divisions of the corporation, while *he* was on the home office staff. When the time came for a new chief executive officer to be appointed, most people thought the division head, as the outstanding line operator in the company, would get the job. But the home office man was closer to the members of the board and he got the job. Both were long-term and devoted employees of the company. But as soon as the staff man got the job, he turned around and, in effect, "killed" his erstwhile opponent. The loser left the company and the company lost a fine man. Either man could have done an excellent job of running this giant company. Such a loss of top management people comes about because big business is holding on to the hierarchical structure and fails to recognize that this structure is, in itself, destructive to the company.

MEMO 16

SIZING UP THE CHIEF EXECUTIVE

The board of directors in a big business already knows a lot about how the president is doing. It meets frequently and receives reports on sales, profits, capital investments, etc. In most large companies the president obviously is not doing everything by himself: the company's other key people are invaluable. A board should know about how the president works with its members and how they work with the president. One way of finding out is to hold a "mock election" and allow all the key people in the company to vote "yes" or "no" or "don't know" on the incumbent president. Inherent in this policy is an openness and a freedom that are compatible with what an increasing number of people in big business want from the corporation. The attitude expressed by such a policy sweeps through a big business organization like a breath of fresh air. Such an attitude gives to the organization much of the same energy, drive, initiative, and imagination that originally were such a powerful force in the free enterprise system. Such an attitude certainly is in direct contrast to the old hierarchical organization with its autocratic and dictatorial approach to management.

Holding a mock election of the president can electrify the people within a company. It will tell them unequivocally what the company stands for, and what the company thinks of them. The best presidents and chief executive officers of big business will welcome it. The most autocratic presidents of big business will reject it out of hand, may even laugh at it. Why? Because it is in fact a significant *symbolic act* that says everything an *innovative* top management wants to say to its people.

There have been some very large and successful businesses built up by the efforts of a single man. Typically such men are dynamic, driven, and autocratic. Their word is law. They are often arbitrary and sometimes cruel. Occasionally they are even unfair. But most of the time they have been right, i.e., they have made things go, and the businesses they have built attest to this. But there are fewer and fewer such men in business. In mature companies they may no longer even be useful. These men are the exception, not the rule, in business today.

If such a man is in charge of a company today, he may do more harm than good. Too much power can, and does, corrupt some men.

Future presidents and other key people leave when the current president gets out of hand and thinks he is an old-fashioned hierarchical autocrat. The board of directors has the legal responsibility to elect the president, and can make certain that such an autocratic attitude on the president's part does not develop. The company must create an environment which will attract and hold talented executives. A person may be a great salesman at the board level, but far less effective in leading and building the executive team of a company. When key people start to leave an organization, the board must find out why. Sales and profits may be going up at the moment of their departures, but this could be changing without being immediately apparent. A company can do well for five years and then begin to fall apart because of inadequate leadership. The time lag between cause and effect is often large in business. Five or six years is not unusual. A president who gets out of hand and loses key personnel may be able to ride through his tenure with rising sales and profits. The effect of the loss of many fine and talented executives during his period may not be fully felt until after he is gone. His successor will then have to spend many unhappy and difficult years in rebuilding.

This does not mean that companies do not need strong leadership. Far from it. Business needs leaders who are forceful and dynamic and who dare to make difficult decisions. But today they must also be honest and democratic in the way they lead. It is the obligation of the board of directors in every business to ascertain that this is the kind of man they have in charge.

Should board members snoop about? Certainly not. Instead, in addition to getting its usual reports, a board should receive reports on the status of key personnel. It should hear from these people directly in meetings at least once a year.

In some cases, a board might find that holding an "election" would also be useful. Certainly such an election is a dramatic action but can be very helpful. It would tell the president what the people think of him *and what they think of how the company is being run.* A mock election of the president has the added advantage of being a tangible expression of the company's respect for the opinions of its key people. It suggests the company is an open, not closed, society in which natural and professional leadership is respected and recognized.

How to conduct such a "mock election"? A notice should be sent out that tells the people specifically about the vote, the purpose of it, and the fundamental philosophy behind it. The announcement would emphasize that this is a serious act, and that the decision and vote of each voter should be made with careful deliberation. The voter should take into consideration all of the pluses and minuses that he or she knows about the president. The voter should try to be as objective and fairminded as possible.

Who should vote in the election? This will vary by company and by situation. Obviously, the people who cast ballots should, to some degree, be knowledgeable about the president. In some companies, all of the executive staff and middle management people might vote. In others, just the executives above the middle management level should vote. In still others, all employees of the company, including executive, administrative, clerical, and production people, should vote.

Once the notice of the election has been sent out, it would be quickly followed by a ballot on which one name would appear: the current president's (or chief executive officer's). There would be three choices: a vote for, or against, or "no comment" on his election for another two-year term. The ballots would be mailed to a special post office box. *No write-in would be permitted.* The ballots would be turned over to the board of directors, and the board of directors and the president alone would have the responsibility for the count and for the report on results.

The board and the president can use this information and make their own judgments. Together, they can accept or reject the vote of the "representatives," but it is certain that they cannot, regardless of their decision, ignore their vote. It is also fair to say that an effective president and board of directors should not be surprised at a vote that gives the president a heavy majority, nor should it be surprised if a weak chief executive gets only a slim majority, or doesn't get a majority at all.

The idea is what is most important here. In some situations, a president may be reluctant to hold an "election," not because he is too autocratic to get on with his key personnel but because he is guiding the company through a difficult period where it can not afford to project a divided image.

As in the British Parliamentary system, the man at the top must have the right to call an "election" when *he* chooses. It must be a genuine agreement between him and the board of directors that it would serve the company's interests.

Even considering the possibility of holding such an election may have an important effect on the president's way of dealing with his executive team. He will review with great care his relations with these people, and decide whether they are in keeping with the open, new management style he knows is best for the company in the long run. If they are not, the best presidents will work to improve them without an "election" being held at all.

"INFORMATION EXCHANGES": A SEMANTIC REVOLUTION

All the various forms of group participation —the committee, the weekly meeting, the special meeting, the all-day meeting, the weekend meeting—have frequently been singled out by critics of big business. It is claimed in committees and meetings there is a loss of individualism which kills individual creativity and individual productivity by robbing a man of his sense of individual accomplishment. Creative people and highly productive people often just give up. They don't believe they can forcefully contribute to a project that is being managed by a group.

I have seen permanent review committees established in a large company with the sole function of reviewing the work of all of the operating people. Over a period of five or six years, these review committees became more and more aggressive, more and more authoritative, and finally oppressive, because the members began to believe that their function was more important than what the operating people were doing. They began to believe they were producing work and not just reviewing it; and, in the end, these permanent committees began to destroy the energy and drive of the operating people. The quality of work suffered. Fortunately, before permanent damage was done, these permanent committees were disbanded, and it was amazing to watch the return of energy and productivity.

We all recognize and can agree that a committee, particularly a permanent one, usually can't accomplish anything of significance. It is not a work-producing mechanism. On the other hand, the very complexity of big business does require that people work cooperatively together to a common purpose—many disciplines are often required to solve a given problem.

Everybody who has been in big business has been on a committee or has been to meetings where very little is achieved. They start slowly. There is too much talk. And there is much talk that is not to the purpose of the meeting. A great deal of time is wasted, and, probably worst of all, people get bored by such activity.

What's the solution?

First, resolve not to ever form a single permanent committee. Make assignments to individuals only. In short, obliterate the word and the thought of a committee from company operations.

Second, add to business some language that takes the onus off meetings and group work. Just as you don't form a committee, don't in effect ever call a "meeting." While this may seem like playing with words, nevertheless, it can have a significant and productive effect within a large organization. When you do get groups together, call such sessions what they really are, *INFORMATION EXCHANGES*, and place one man in charge.

For example, an information exchange is called by Godfrey, with Smith, O'Donald, Fabius, and Grunwalde attending. The starting time is 10:00 A.M. The stopping time is 11:00 A.M. or earlier. The subject is a new product by the competition. Godfrey runs the meeting. He starts it. He controls the time. He controls the discussion. He ends the information exchange. He decides what will be presented. He decides what will be discussed. He is responsible for doing anything that needs to be done as a result of this information exchange. He is responsible for drawing any conclusions that come from the information exchange. He is responsible for the decisions and actions that result. It may be that Godfrey will make an additional assignment regarding information. He may call another information exchange in follow-up to the first one before deciding he can make an intelligent and productive decision. Everyone at the exchange knows Godfrey is the man who will make a decision. They know they can influence his decision with information. Each has his own job to do and his own area of responsibility, and the subject that Godfrey has brought to them is his subject and his area of concentration and his area of responsibility.

There are many big businesses that spend thousands and thousands of manpower hours in meetings and in work on committees. More often than not these committees only produce reports but not much in the way of significant action and results. Replacing them with "information exchanges" will prove not only more productive but economical as well.

MEMO 18

NEW VENTURE COMPANIES: CHEAP GROWTH FOR FUN AND PROFIT

This is not a totally new idea nor is it completely original, but it has immense appeal for new managers, and is compatible with the breakdown of the hierarchical structure of big business.

Already new venture capital programs have been set up by Standard Oil of New Jersey, Dow Chemical, Singer, American Can, Hercules, and General Electric.

Installing new venture capital units within a company provides a specific and tangible method for producing *internal* growth but, at the same time, permits a company to reach out into new product areas and new industries that in effect become a form of external growth without having to resort to the much more expensive and much more difficult use of acquisitions to achieve these objectives.

New venture capital units that do succeed and do produce added sales volume and added profit can make a significant contribution over the years to earnings per share growth since there will be little or no dilution in the stock ownership.

New venture capital units will attract some of the best entrepreneurs from within a company and from the outside, because these units give such men a chance to fully exploit their energies and talents to create and build businesses within the framework of existing big business. These new units can give to the entire corporation a spirit of vitality, action, and drive that is contagious.

In mature industries a new venture capital unit can be invaluable in helping a company produce dynamic new growth. In such industries the products, the major competitors, and the distribution channels are well established. Consumers are familiar with the trade names (if there are trade names). There is consistent demand and use of the products within the industry. In such industries growth tends to follow population growth patterns. The only opportunity for accelerated growth that can exceed normal population growth must be achieved by getting a greater share of the market. This takes time and a great deal of money; and often this type of growth, because it is costly, produces a lower margin of profit for the company.

In recent years companies in such mature industries which sought dynamic growth have found a solution through acquisitions. Thus in the nineteen sixties, the conglomerate idea was fully developed and exploited. But it is fair to say that the conglomerate idea has only been partially successful. The experience of conglomerates has shown again and again that this method of external growth is not without serious problems. The more diverse the expansion in external growth, the more disparate the companies acquired, the more potential there is for trouble.

Acquisitions can also be very expensive. Often there is very little immediate gain in earnings per share. There may be growth in sales and dollar profit, but this does not represent real equity growth. Typically, aside from "outstanding bargains," acquisitions take two, three, four years to make significant increases in earnings per share.

The establishment of venture capital units is an alternate way to achieve external growth with far less risk and far less expense. Venture capital units can permit a large company to slip into new markets without a great deal of fanfare. Of course, not every venture capital unit will be successful and productive. Unavoidably, there will be a fairly high attrition rate. But investments in new venture capital units will be relatively minor. At the same time, there are opportunities for success that can be most rewarding.

General Electric's wholly owned subsidiary is called "Business Development Services, Inc." and it was set up in the late nineteen sixties. It is probably the biggest and most active of all the corporate venture groups, has twenty-five per cent to forty per cent interest in each of a dozen small companies, and has invested seven million dollars of the twenty-five million dollar venture capital fund established by GE.

GE went into the business in search of growth areas that are related to the current GE business but not directly in line with current products. This gives the GE venture capital program a very large spectrum in which to work. So far GE venture capital products include: artificial human organs, reactors for manufacturing integrated circuits and semiconductors, plastic extrusions and coatings, analytical instrumentation systems, three-dimensional electronic drafting devices, and a speech synthesizer that would enable computers to talk. GE hopes to develop some of these companies to a point where they will want to take over the entire company. In short, the GE program is a combination of venture capital investments and acquisitions. It is their hope that GE can develop out of every ten such ventures three that will become big enough to become new divisions of the business and, in the process, become very helpful to GE's long-term growth.

The GE venture capital program is managed by men who have worked in the venture capital field before. They are experienced in investing and also in making the judgments on which ventures to go into. The program is

long-term and they are looking for major results five years ahead. This program is
immensely attractive to inventive and innovative entrepreneurs who want to start their own
business and who have a bright idea but lack
both the capital to get started and some of the
technical support that is necessary to develop
high technology products of this type. In this
connection, once a company has been given
GE venture capital, there is practically no
limit to the technical help it can get; and GE's
own research labs become available along
with a wealth of other information that probably would not be available to a company
operating completely on its own. GE even
provides recommendations on international
financing and marketing. In short, the GE venture capital program provides capital, management skills, marketing skills, and access to
top engineers and scientists in some of the
world's best research and development
laboratories.

GE believes its venture capital program is
bound to increase in the future because for a
relatively modest investment such ventures
can open up some important areas of development in new products and new tech-
nologies.

Standard Oil of New Jersey has a similar
attitude. They know that it is difficult for anyone to predict what the great new industries of
the future are going to be. At the same time,
they do know that Jersey Standard wants to be

in on those industries, whatever they are; so they have set up a venture capital program to get into new and different activities outside the normal oil and gas focus. Jersey Standard has started up four venture capital companies in recent years: one making computer memory systems, one working on a speech system for computers, one developing new types of rechargeable batteries, and one using a new process to manufacture fine wire.

All of the venture capital programs are not necessarily involved in high technology work. American Can has new venture units working on packaging, consumer research, and specialty chemicals. Dow Chemical has an Alaskan housing venture, and Singer has venture capital units in the fast-growing health food field and a massive industrial real estate project on the Texas Gulf Coast.

I have observed that more than twenty companies have set up special staffs to make new capital ventures, and scores of others, including some of the biggest, are now doing planning work in this area. Most of the venture capital companies spawned by big business have been in operation for only three years, and, typically, it takes five to seven years before such ventures can be determined successful.

There can be no set pattern for establishing new venture capital units, but there are some steps that can and should be taken in sequence. These follow the pattern of what companies have done that have been successful in setting up new venture capital units.

The first step is to set up a preliminary venture capital fund as part of a basic corporate budget. The size of this fund depends upon the company and the nature of the industry and the types of ventures that are anticipated. This preliminary fund need only represent some seed money to get this idea started because it is impractical to establish a basic venture capital fund before doing a great deal of specific work to determine the objectives for the various venture capital units.

Once the preliminary fund is established, then a broad range of objectives can be formulated by top management for the venture capital program. In most cases these objectives will define the industries or the product areas for the new ventures. These objectives will be broad-based and will not be so specific as to restrict the work that is to follow.

The next step is to get the people inside and outside the company who are interested in establishing and building new ventures. The selection of these people is the most important action taken by top management. The right people are very often the key factor in making a new venture capital program work. They must be innovators. They must be creative, and imaginative, and energetic. Top management that really does know its middle management people on an intimate basis will have little difficulty in selecting the right ones to head up the new venture capital units. Typically, these people will be found in research, in engineering, in marketing, and in sales.

Ideally, each venture capital unit will have two or three people involved, and together they will complement each other. An imaginative, driving, energetic leader may need a sound, sensible, good-judgment person as a partner to give balance to the effort.

Once a venture capital team is set up, it uses the overall corporate objectives to establish specific areas of opportunity for the development of their new venture. The plan that is produced for the venture capital unit will clearly define the market to be reached, the product or service to be developed, and the amount of investment required. This will take three to six months at a minimum and will involve extensive study and research. A timetable for product development and production should be included, and a schedule of sales objectives developed. Finally, some profit objectives have to be set.

When the plan has been developed, presented to top management and accepted (or refined if necessary), then the venture capital unit should be formally established. It should be given identity via a corporate name and set up as a separate operating unit with its own staff. Most important, it should set up operations in its own building separate from corporate headquarters.

Each new venture capital unit will, of

course, have to draw on an established venture capital fund according to a schedule established by the three-year plan. Each new venture capital unit should report monthly on its progress, and every six months should present any refinement or basic change required in the overall plan as a result of its experience to date.

Management must not expect that every venture capital unit will be a success. There have to be some failures. But for the successes, the rewards will be great; the successes will produce the best kind of growth. There will be "external" growth that is, in fact, internal, and it will be all plus.

A venture capital unit will attract an exciting breed of innovative and imaginative people. A new venture capital program will permit the company to hold on to the best and most dynamic people within the organization. Venture capital units can help big business make optimum use of one of its most valuable assets: the creative and restless and imaginative minds of its very best people.

MEMO 19

DARE TO BE WRONG!

After you have been inside a big business for a while, it is important to remind yourself of its fallibility. The "perfection of the enterprise" is something that won't strike you immediately, but it will eventually become apparent in many subtle ways and some not so subtle ways. You notice it in the talk of the people within a big business. You notice it in the advertising, the public relations releases, and the memos and bulletins. Although a form of positive thinking, it ultimately convinces the people within a big company that they live and work in a perfect world.

The company is always right. The performance of management people is close to perfection. They have made no mistakes and are not likely to in the future. To be sure, there are problems, but the problems are not created on the inside. They are the result of competition or the state of the industry. This attitude may even prevail when a big company is getting into serious trouble.

I have listened to top management men in dozens and dozens of big businesses, and I have rarely heard a top management man openly say to outsiders and to his associates that the company "really blew that one," or admit that he personally has made a major mistake in judgment.

It has reached the point where even test products that bomb are presented in a positive light. For example, a new floor wax was test-marketed in three markets. After the required time period, the returns on the new product came in, and they were terrible. But when the presentation was made the emphasis was placed on how effectively and efficiently the test market program had been run, and how clearly it showed that the company should not proceed with this particular product. Perhaps the people who conducted the test marketing were properly proud of the way they had done their job. But the fact was, the product had performed so poorly that a more accurate judgment prior to the marketing program should have indicated that this particular product didn't have much of a chance. Obviously, a serious mistake in judgment had been made in spending something like over $300,000 on the product and on the three test markets.

There are, of course, some very specific reasons for this attitude. First, the size of the average big business. Performance in sales and profits when viewed by the individual can be literally staggering. There is the growth record over twenty, thirty, or forty years. Look at the sales. Look at the profits. You have to come to the conclusion that the company has been incredibly clever. Just look at that home office building. Often it is new, and big, and modern, and impressive. Look at the people who run the company. Observe their enthusiasm and confidence and positiveness. Then look at the plans for the future. In short, the size, the growth, and the success of many big businesses say all that needs to be said. Here is the strength, efficiency, and talent that add up to something close to perfection.

Another reason can be found in the hierarchical organization. The men at the top are royalty and the very top man is king: he carries about him an air of infallibility. He has enormous power, and to maintain it he can't afford to make mistakes, and he can't afford to admit mistakes. In the hierarchical organization, men at the top of the pyramid, and the men at the top of all the sub-pyramids maintain their positions, in part, through this attitude. They look right, and they are right. They rarely look backward. Everything is "onward and upward." It's part of their job to maintain an attitude and style that will help to keep all the people who are working under them in a positive frame of mind. The hierarchic organizational structure requires this degree of perfection in order to maintain itself.

Men who are climbing to the top of a hierarchical organization can't admit to mistakes. It just isn't done. The competition within the organization for promotion is such that the man who goes around openly talking, not only about his successes, but also about his mistakes, will soon find that he has produced a negative image. His competition is always waiting for the other man to make a mistake. Most successful pyramid climbers in big business learn not to take big chances. They learn to be cautious and conservative, and they learn to keep their mouths shut when things do go wrong. The successful climber in big business has to create a "no-mistake" image.

The size of big business tends to hide mistakes. The time lag, from idea to plan to action and to results, is often three or four years. Over such a long period of time, who is to say who did what and when he did it? Even in the fast-moving packaged goods industry, three years is not untypical for the development of an idea into a new product through to the final results. In addition, most of the programs that are put in place in big business require a contribution by a wide variety of disciplines; so it is hard to define failures and it is hard to pin down who is responsible for failures—in effect, then, there are none.

In summary, the factors of size, hierarchy, competition within the organization, lead time, and job fractionation, all tend to hide the errors and in a sense to "dissolve" the mistakes of big business, thus producing the environment of perfection.

Obviously, this is not good for big business. It produces attitudes in men that are unrealistic. The company apparently demands of its key people a level of performance that is so mistake-free and close to perfection that it isn't at all possible. So the next best thing for the man to do is to appear to be perfect. The simple-minded advocates of positive thinking may do better, but, even while they talk positive, they are cautious and they make sure they don't make *obvious* mistakes.

The result is that too many men in big business who have made a total commitment to the company are not similarly committed to their actions, to the job that has to be done. There are not enough men who take an idea and turn it into a plan and an action with a sense of total commitment, who have a clear understanding that there is a possibility of failure, and that, in the plan and in the action, the man himself stands to rise or fall.

The caution that Perfection induces is an impediment to innovation. It tends to make people seek the middle of the road rather than the far-out reaches. It tends to make people approach a project and an idea with caution and to select the safest option with the minimum amount of risk. Men in big business have found that too much aggressiveness and too much creative effort can be dangerous.

They know that it works sometimes, but for the career man dedicated to the idea of making the long climb in a company, it can be dangerous.

The Perfection of big business creates a false attitude of positiveness, which is damaging. We all know that to grow, to innovate, you have to do a lot of things right, but in the process you are bound to do some things wrong.

Perfection in big business is driving the innovators out of big business. They don't like what happens to their ideas. They don't like what happens to their efforts to innovate. The caution that is too often a part of big business dampens the creative spirit.

What should big business do about this? One basic organization change has to be made: get rid of the hierarchical organization structure and, in the process, get rid of the caution that this type of organization produces in the men in big business.

Big business has to give more responsibility to more people, and it has to give more people more freedom to act, to produce, to report, to succeed, and to fail. Big business has to recognize that Perfection can be destructive. Big business has to recognize that it needs some failures to produce outstanding successes. And big business has to recognize that it needs more outstanding successes to keep up in what is an increasingly competitive business world.

MEMO 20

IN-HOUSE REBEL: THE MODERN MANAGER

It isn't always easy to get something done in a big business. The problems that impede a person's ability to produce results are often significant enough to force him to leave big business. It is easy to come to the conclusion that, no matter how hard you work and no matter what you do, you just can't get the kind of job satisfaction that can only come from tangible achievement.

Management people in big business must learn how to fight the organization if they are to be effective. They must adopt methods of management that are appropriate only to big business. They must rethink their jobs and approach them differently from their predecessors.

In big business it often takes a very long time from the inception of an idea to evaluation, to the plan of action, to the actual action, and, finally, to the end result. This is a characteristic of bigness.

Working within the organization and within the vertical organization structure that exists in many big companies can be difficult. There are too many people in big business just along for the ride. They don't care about producing results. It's as if they were working in the post office. Security is the primary motivation.

Big business is drowning in a flood of paper. Reports, memoranda for the record, etc., are glutting the communication channels and have produced an attitude among many big business people that all this paper work is really getting the job done. In its simplest terms, big business is people making things and selling things, or people providing services and selling services; and, while these people have to be knowledgeable about what they are doing and trained in what they are doing, the paper they get each day is not in any way a substitute for getting the job done.

Committees grow like weeds in big business. In every department and in every division, there are committees. But all that talking usually fails to produce results.

People in big business become isolated from the outside world. They spend so much time working within the organization that they know little else, which can be stifling.

All of these "problems" in big business, from lead time to inherent complexity, to the difficulty of working within the organization, to the paper flood, the committees, and the isolation, produce for the people in big business a major and basic problem. Individual effort and the results that are eventually produced are often completely separated. When you have a person working under these conditions, he lacks enthusiasm because he lacks a feeling of accomplishment.

What is the solution? Every big business manager must revamp his attitudes and act on them.

The successful big business manager of the future will have no delusions about the conditions that exist within big business. He recognizes all of the problems I have specified in these memoranda and he fights back. He *has* to fight to make the most effective use of his time.

A manager can be pulled in a hundred different directions by the people within the organization. The modern big business manager must not allow the organization to run him. He controls the use of his time carefully. He refuses to waste time on nonessential functions or functions of secondary importance. He plots his days and weeks and years to permit him to concentrate on the major jobs that have to be done. He plans his day so that he doesn't spend five minutes on one job, ten minutes on another, five minutes on another, twenty minutes on another. If the job is worth doing, it is worth spending *enough* time on. How much is enough time? There can be no hard and fast guideline. But the point is that it often happens that the manager's time in big business is fractionated to the point where he does a lot of everything, but gets little or nothing done. The successful manager in big business spends a lot of time with people, for instance. He knows that only with time can he make the right decisions about people.

He shouldn't worry about being criticized because he doesn't do everything. He doesn't worry about being criticized because a certain amount of his paper work is not reviewed or responded to or even read. He doesn't worry because some people say of him (within the organization) that he doesn't do this little thing or that little thing effectively. What he worries about is making sure that what he does do, he spends enough time on to be sure that he does it well. Probably one of the biggest differences between small business and big business is this matter of time management. In small business there is usually just one major job to do and there is plenty of time to concentrate on it. The organization is small enough to prevent the fractionating of time. But in big business the demands on time are tremendous, and the conscientious person can overreact and overrespond to every demand and, finally, have his day broken up into five-minute segments that, in the long run, produce a kind of emotional exhaustion and very little in the way of tangible and specific results for the company and for himself.

The effective manager in big business doesn't just give orders; he has long since learned that the authoritarian method of managing does not work. He knows that if he is going to get a job done, he must *contribute* to that job and he must contribute in a specific and tangible way. When there is a job to be done, he pitches in and works with the other people who are working for him. He contributes by specific action to the job and, through that specific action, he contributes a form of leadership that is stimulating and productive to his fellow workers. When a person works in this way, he automatically brings to the job a completely different attitude from his predecessors cut from the old authoritarian mold. He really does feel that he is responsible for results and he really does hold himself accountable for these results.

A person who works in this way may be tough, and he may be hard-driving, and he may be demanding; but almost always he is honest and fair with his people. Perhaps this is the most important trait of the new and successful manager in big business. He sees himself as a co-contributor and a co-worker. Usually he has more experience and talent than some of his other co-workers. But because he is working *with* his people, he has learned that he must be fair and honest with them if he is going to get their maximum effort and support.

He is a good communicator. He keeps people informed because he knows that when they are well informed they know not only how to do what they are doing, but why they are doing it; and this is a significant source of motivation. He is continuously developing the talents and strengths of his fellow workers and, in the process, developing and enlarging his own strengths.

The successful manager knows his own strengths and weaknesses. He knows from experience and from what people have told him and by objective evaluation what he can't do at all or what he can't do very well. He must know which areas he should stay away from. With this knowledge he is able to develop a clear understanding of his own strengths. The idea of the well-rounded person who does a little bit of everything is old-fashioned. We don't need him today. He may do a little bit of everything, but he doesn't do one or two or even three things in an outstanding fashion. The well-rounded individual doesn't just build on strengths. What he does do is take away from his natural strengths by trying to compensate for his weaknesses. If a person is an exceptional salesman, he should sell. Even when he gets to be a member of top management of the company, he should continue to employ his greatest strengths for himself and for the company.

The philosophy of the contributing leader working within the area of his maximum strength is what big business needs more of today. This is the new way to manage. Big business has the responsibility of tailoring jobs to fit people rather than the other way around. This means that the old approach of using job descriptions has to be junked. You don't build an organization with a bunch of job descriptions and then just fill the job descriptions with people. You build an organization with people who have an opportunity to exploit, develop, and build on their strengths. You recognize that a job function may change when a new person comes in to work in a particular area, and welcome it. He may not be the same kind of a person as his predecessor; he may have different strengths, and that's okay too.

The successful big business recognizes the need to build on strengths, and in the process it tolerates weaknesses. Not that these weaknesses are ignored by the people who work within big business. But if they are understood they can be compensated for effectively by the organization in order to give to each man a maximum opportunity to build on strengths and to grow.

The effective manager in big business thinks through his job and he gives it rank order priorities. He decides that there are one, or two, or three, or four major things that he has to do, and then he ignores, to a large degree, most of the smaller jobs. He accepts the idea that he will be criticized within the organization, and perhaps outside of the organization, because he doesn't do everything well and he doesn't get everything done; but what he does do well is very, very important, and what he does get done contributes significantly to the success of the company. When he decides on those things that come first, he does this with an eye to the future, and he does this with the thought that, by producing some action and results in these high-priority functions, he can make a significant contribution to that future. He works largely in the area of opportunities, rather than problems. There are many problems that develop in big business that can't be solved no matter how much work and effort are applied.

When it comes to decisions, the successful big business manager *fights* the organization. He doesn't try to make every decision. If he wants to seek out all his potential decision-making opportunities, he can find literally hundreds and thousands of them during the course of the year. But the successful manager stays away from those decisions that he is not directly involved with. He doesn't make a lot of decisions. He makes a few of them. Just a few. But the decisions that he does make are decisions that determine basic strategy for his job and that affect and influence the future. And his decisions include actions. In other words, if a decision is made to do something, then the specific action that must take place is also defined.

The effective decision-maker decides what is the right thing to do, the best thing to do, and then takes a little bit off it by compromise, because compromise is almost always necessary. The effective decision-maker always gets a clear set of objectives of the problem or the job before making a decision. He knows the numbers; he knows the height and width, the depth and the weight of the thing that has to be moved before he decides on whether or not to move it, or how to move it.

The effective manager works for results. That's his reward and the company's reward. And how does he find out what the results are? He does the checking himself. And why does he check himself? Because he has already been involved in the job; he has been a contributor; and it's an easy thing for him to go one step further and check and evaluate exactly what has been achieved.

The effective decision-maker knows that there are three ways to approach a decision: he decides to do something; he decides not to do something; or he decides not to decide at all, but merely to delay the decision. It is important to note that delaying the decision, or not deciding, is in itself a decision. This is done consistently by the man who wants to make just a few big decisions and make them right.

You can see from what I have said the effective manager in big business today fights the organization. He doesn't try to destroy it. He recognizes the inherent weaknesses of big business and he fights it in order to prevent the transferral of its inherent weaknesses to himself. He knows how to value his time, and when he uses it, he uses it in big chunks. He contributes to a job rather than merely orders that it be done, and he does so with his known strengths. He doesn't try to do everything, doesn't try to be everywhere. He concentrates his time and his effort and he does first things first.

MEMO 21

FIGHTING THE ORGANIZATION: A DUTY AND A RIGHT

Everyone in big business should fight big business, but not with a destructive objective. There is no point in telling the boss to go to hell because there's always another boss. There is also no point in dropping out to be a farmer. If you are in an organization now you have to succumb or resist, try to change it or quit. Every decision you face on the problem of the individual versus authority is something of a dilemma. It isn't a case of whether you should fight back against tyranny or blaze a new trail against the hierarchy. The real issue is much more subtle. For the person in big business, it isn't the evils of business life that produce his problem, but its very benevolence. All too often, he is made to feel he is part of a brotherhood.

People do have to work with others, and a well-functioning team is a whole lot greater than the sum of its parts. It is precisely because this is an age of big business that the other side of the coin needs to be emphasized. We need to know how to work within big business but, at the same time, to resist it and to change it. History has taught us that philosophical individualism can venerate conflict too much and cooperation too little. The energies of Americans have been devoted to a cooperative effort in big business, and these efforts, as I said earlier in the book, are not to be demeaned. The more power big business has over the individual, the more he needs to recognize where he must fight against it. Big business has been created by men and can be changed by them. It has not been the immutable course of history that has produced the constrictions of big business. It is the management man who has brought them to pass and it is he who can stop them. But too many people within the organization worship it. Too many people today see themselves as objects, more acted upon than acting; and their future therefore is determined as much by the system of big business as by themselves.

It is true that in a society or in an organization individualism can be carried to such an extreme as to endanger the organization itself. It is true that in extreme cases individualism can be corrupted into a narrow egoism which prohibits effective cooperation. At the same time, it is essential to recognize the danger from a climate which by inhibiting individual initiative and imagination can be destructive to the organization that produces that climate.

Big business has overemphasized the importance of getting along with others. In fact, a considerable body of literature has been produced on this subject. At times the "preaching" has reached a fever pitch and the pitchman emerges as a sort of pied piper, carrying the big company's banner. There is too much emphasis on the well-rounded person in our time. He does a little bit of everything and not a lot of any one thing. People shouldn't just cooperate; they should cooperate for a substantive reason to achieve goals; and unless these goals are clearly understood, the manipulations that helped produce team spirit and high morale and getting along can be, in the long run, destructive to the individual.

The skills that are used to produce cooperative effort can easily tempt a manager into the practice of a new form of tyranny, more subtle than that of his entrepreneurial predecessor, but at the same time more dangerous, because his attitudes and positions and directives are not as straight forward and as clear and as blunt as that of the autocrat-owner.

There are few things that are more calculated to take away from the individual his identity than the idea that his interests and those interests of the organization can be totally compatible. In a good organization there must be cooperation and there has to be a high degree of compatibility between the organization's and the individual's interests, but they can never be completely the same.

144

Once the individual allows the organization to decide what is most important, he ultimately sacrifices himself. In the business organization of the future, there must be much more encouragement of individual expression. The organization structure itself should and must be formed to Human Measure.

MEMO 22

INTRODUCING THE NEW BUSINESS GENERATION

What people want and need from their work is
changing. It is clear that the so-called "Organization Man" of the nineteen fifties and his
slightly modified brother of the nineteen sixties are fast disappearing from the business
scene. The Organization Man was reconciled
to his role of serving big companies. He wasn't
particularly concerned with preserving his
individuality and he was willing to go along
with management toward goals the companies judged valid. Typically, he was well
educated, pragmatic, zealous, and absorbed in
his company to the exclusion of almost everything else. He had no interest in changing corporate life or corporate goals, and he almost
never doubted the worth of these goals nor the
worth and importance of his role. Some people in big business today are quite different
from the Organization Man. They reflect a
passionate concern for individuality, openness, humanness, and change. They are determined to be heard.

"I went there in 1965 because it looked like good pay and a good chance for advancement. Those were my goals then. But I felt like a small cog. Working there was dehumanizing and the struggle to get to the top didn't seem worth it. They made no effort to encourage your participation. The decisions were made in those rooms with closed doors. You didn't know how you were doing. The company didn't tell you you were important . . . perhaps because they were afraid you would want more money. The serious error made with me was not giving me a glimpse of the big picture from time to time so I could go back to my little detail, understanding how it related to the whole. I was just left there. When I told my boss why I was quitting he didn't understand. He'd been in it twenty years; he told me he'd gone through it all. While I stuck it out, I was playing the game. I had the money and the car and the apartment, all the tinsel. But I felt I wasn't giving anything. Only two percent of me was being used."

Many people in big business today have plenty of ideas about what needs changing and are spelling them out to their companies with increasing frankness. Their interests center around personal and psychological values, not material ones. *They rarely show much concern about fringe benefits.* This is partly because such long-range defensive thinking is foreign to their conception of themselves. A fundamental requirement is responsibility. People in business want the responsibility to make real decisions—and real mistakes—because they believe that's the only way to learn and make progress.

"The management-achievement program gives men responsibility almost immediately. I had responsibility in the military service, with seventy-five people under me, and I wanted a job with good gravity, one that was important to the company. I was assigned to determine whether a proposed new tape drive for data processing equipment would pose any operational problems. I held a ten-week trial, made a favorable recommendation, and after further evaluations, over three million dollars' worth of tape drives were bought."

"I have responsibility for the advertising programs for ten of the bank's corporate departments, coordinating their ads with the bank's overall marketing strategy, and supervising budgets. Around here they give you all the responsibility you can handle and all the rope you need to hang yourself. It's very exciting."

"I would like to be in on the decision making. This is part of my life style. This is the kind of change organizations of the future must make in order to operate in a new environment in this new participatory democracy."

"I have a questioning attitude. I won't accept the status quo and I won't accept irrational behavior on the part of management. I have a concern for the long-range implications of company policies, beyond the traditional attention to quarter-to-quarter results. If I don't have a say in setting goals, and don't agree that those goals are correct, then I don't have a commitment to do the job."

"I don't mind coming in early or staying late, but I won't stay late just to write status reports that no one reads. I don't like going through layers and layers of bureaucracy. I don't like the unnecessary paper work they cause. And I'm not afraid to tell my supervisor I don't have time to do something."

"I wanted responsibility and growth, not so much for the money, but for the chance to have authority and a real voice in company decisions. I wanted to operate on my own without someone peering over my shoulder. Within reason I want autonomy and the freedom to make mistakes. I couldn't get it and so I left. If you stifle people, you are going to lose them."

Many of the personal concerns expressed by people in business center around the extent to which they are treated as individuals. There is a need for big business to put emphasis on personal recognition. People need attachments for growth, and they attach themselves to people, to objects, to ideas, and to organizations. They really do want to latch on to companies, but only if they can be effective, solve problems, and look good to themselves.

"I interviewed with a railroad. They were a bunch of guys with little railroad things on their ties. You were bound to think that if you stuck there you would have a helluva job if you were patient because everybody around was a clod."

"I object to the idea of the company attempting to impose an arbitrary pattern on my life. This includes not only the ritual transfer to a distant city, but also the feeling that I have to 'put in my time' or 'pay my dues' before any authority can be given to me."

"I was hired by the numbers. There was a fixed routine, and chances of breaking it were slim indeed. I would have had to go through the whole pattern, which might have taken a thousand years. I left instead."

"In designing a new plant they determined to make the factory seem like a collection of small units, rather than one vast impersonal building. This feeling for scale, or Human Measure, is appreciated by people. They praise the 'small company atmosphere' in which staffs are kept as lean as possible. They tend to give a man total responsibility and to give him an opportunity to fail in order to grow."

"I dislike conspicuous display of the trappings of power . . . the six-button telephones, the pompous titles, the thick carpets and the fancy furniture . . . if these things are only empty tokens. I will not be governed by rules covering my dress or the enforcement of rigid hours where a looser schedule would work, not only as well, but probably would make me more productive."

"The old way of bringing people in at the bottom and hoping the cream will rise doesn't work any more. You have to handcraft jobs for people and put them under a good manager and watch carefully, so the older people don't kill off the young ones by demanding years of experience before letting them tackle a meaningful job."

Big business has been late in coming to the idea of accommodating people. Big business has to pay serious, dignified attention to individuals, and it will stand or fall on how this job is handled in the future. The ethic of today is to contribute. The best way to keep the ablest of people in big business is to load them a little beyond their capacity. That capacity can turn out to be very high, to the benefit of both the individual and the big business he works for.

MEMO 23

BOOKS YOU SHOULD ALREADY KNOW

One of the earliest books on big business was written by Adolph A. Berle and Gardiner C. Means in 1932, *The Modern Corporation and Private Property* (Harcourt, Brace & World, New York: 1932). It contains a profound analysis of the then growing separation of the ownership of business and control of business and the extent to which share ownership was becoming more dispersed. It includes insights into many of the problems that big business faces today. Berle and Means suggested that the consolidation of corporations into larger and larger units was a process that would probably continue indefinitely, and that, since the managers of the corporation were not the owners, it was unlikely that they would be concerned solely with maximizing the return on shareholders' capital.

In 1933 Joan Robinson, in Britain, and E. H. Chamberlain, in the U.S., published books providing new theoretical models which recognized that the characteristic form of market structure was somewhere between the two limiting extremes of pure competition and pure monopoly. Joan Robinson called her book *The Economics of Imperfect Competition* (Macmillan, London: 1933), while Chamberlain called his *Theory of Monopolistic Competition* (Harvard University Press, Boston: 1933). Both books emphasized the imperfect nature of competition in our economy, with particular emphasis on the effects of big business.

Joseph Schumpeter, whose book *Capitalism, Socialism and Democracy* (George Allen & Unwin, London) was published in 1943, saw clearly the evolutionary nature of the capitalistic system. He saw it as one in which creative destruction is an essential fact. He foresaw the private ownership of firms evolving into the publicly owned companies and of small organizations being swallowed up by larger ones. Schumpeter's argument was that large units were necessary to exploit modern technology and that competition would continue, if not in price, in terms of organizational efficiency.

William Baumol and Robert Marris, in *The Economic Theory of Managerial Capitalism* (Macmillan, London: 1964), completely reworked the theory of the firm maintaining that big business was overwhelmingly managerial. The theory of the firm was based on the assumption that managers are concerned primarily with the growth of their firm, security, and a reasonable return to shareholders. They also indicated that consumers' interests, in terms of product quality, prices, and innovation, were threatened by this new "managerial" capitalism.

John Kenneth Galbraith's *The New Industrial State* (Houghton Mifflin, Boston: 1967) in many ways sums up much that has been said about the characteristics and problems of big business. In two previous books, *American Capitalism* (Penguin Books, London: 1963) and *The Affluent Society* (Houghton Mifflin, Boston: 1958), Galbraith drew attention to some of the dramatic new features of the society, notably the juxtaposition of monopolistic sellers with monopolistic buyers.

The New Industrial State went a lot further. In this book Galbraith destroys completely the role of the market in determining the allocation of resources and, hence, of sovereignty of the consumer. The market, with its competitive pressures toward the public good has, he argues, been replaced by the judgment of managers or, as he defines them, the "technostructure." The objective of the technostructure is the continued growth and security of the corporation, an endeavor which the government is obliged to support whether it wants to or not and which is a necessity of modern technology. He seems to think that on economic matters the technostructure is beneficent, infallible, and indispensable.

The problems and awareness of these problems are not new. Far from it. In fact, what Berle and Means said in 1932, Galbraith said again in 1967. What these critics of our system of big business are saying can be summarized as follows:

• Big business creates a lack of competition or destroys it completely. Within some industries, a monopoly exists and in others an oligarchy. Over a period of time the big companies in an industry get bigger and stronger and, eventually, either absorb or destroy the smaller companies.

• Big business is inefficient. In contrast to the general assumption, size does not necessarily produce greater economies in production. In fact, a recent study indicates that maximum efficiency in plant size is achieved when the plant can produce twenty per cent of automobiles, twenty-two per cent of typewriters, five per cent of soap, and two per cent of flour. Yet in many of these industries, some of the big companies have much larger shares than those indicated and merely have a multiplicity of plants to fulfill their share of the market.

• There is too much growth for the sake of growth. In the last twenty years, corporate expenditures on acquisitions have risen from less than five per cent of new corporate investment to over fifty per cent. In 1967 there were three thousand mergers; in 1968, four thousand five hundred; and in 1969, five thousand. Much of this growth by acquisition does not produce greater efficiency or better products or lower prices.

- Big business has joined forces with big government. The result is that in some industries, particularly those related to defense or air transportation or space exploration, the share of sales to government grows and grows. Some big business can't do without big government and vice versa.

- Ownership in big business has lost control. It is now in the hands of professional management. (There isn't any disagreement about this.) Annual stockholder meetings are for purposes of show only. It is a rare annual meeting that is a significant event and that in any way influences the operation of the company. The proxy statement is the legal device used by management to control big business.

- Big business doesn't serve the consumer or the owners; it serves, instead, the management that runs big business.

Someone has said that big and bad tend to go together, that bigness leads to badness, and that nothing should be any bigger than it has to be. This is the kind of idea that excites people, and it gets printed and talked about. But it is meaningless unless adequate alternatives to bigness are also provided. As far as the people in big business are concerned, this is what I have tried to do in this book.

Confrontation
in psychotherapy
with the alcoholic

Consulting Editor
Alcohol and Drug Studies
Robert J. Ackerman
Indiana University of Pennsylvania

Confrontation
in psychotherapy
with the alcoholic

Gary G. Forrest, Ph.D.

with Foreword by

Arthur P. Knauert, M.D.

LEARNING PUBLICATIONS, INC.
Holmes Beach, Florida

ISBN: 0-918452-32-5

Co-Editors:
  Edsel L. Erickson
  Lois A. Carl

Learning Publications, Inc.
P.O. Box 1326
Holmes Beach, FL 33509

Cover Design by Melinda Frink Kabel

Printing: 3 4 5 6 7 8   Year: 5 6 7

Printed in the United States of America

ACKNOWLEDGMENTS

Many have contributed directly or indirectly to this work. Foremost in this respect are my wife Sandra and my daughters Sarah Ellen and Allison. Their love, support and encouragement provided me with the strength needed to complete the manuscript. My secretary, Mrs. Eileen Moorhead, has been most helpful and encouraging. Finally, as always, I must thank my patients. Without our mutual sharing during hundreds of hours of therapy, I would lack the clinical experience, concern and wisdom essential to writing about the process of psychotherapy with alcoholic persons.

CONTENTS

FOREWORD

In order to work successfully with alcoholic clients it is necessary to understand the maneuvers they use to maintain their drinking. It is imperative that the clinician develop techniques to counteract these maneuvers. In this short, but important work, Dr. Forrest explores one such technique, confrontation. Confrontation can be highly effective in breaking through the reality distortions that alcoholics use in order to continue drinking.

Confrontation can be understood as a method of juxtaposing two differing views of reality and thus focusing attention on the distortion of the client's perception that allows him or her to continue to drink and behave alcoholically. This procedure is extremely helpful in overcoming denial, one of the major defenses of the alcoholic.

It may at first seem surprising that an alcoholic can report that physical health, job effectiveness, interpersonal interactions and emotional well-being have all been negatively affected by drinking and still deny the presence of alcoholism. However, if it is appreciated that without denial it would be significantly harder to take the first drink, denial can then be viewed as a maneuver which the client utilizes in order to avoid facing reality and the sobriety that reality implies.

As Dr. Forrest points out, confrontation can be hurtful and harmful to the client or, if presented in a caring manner, extremely beneficial. Counselors should develop their own style and technique of confrontation in

therapy with alcoholic clients. Dr. Forrest's book will be very helpful in this regard. A method I have found effective in this realm is the "Recognizing a Duck" technique. After eliciting the history of the effects of drinking on the client and having the client deny alcoholism, I often tell the following story.

A friend of mine, an outdoorsman, once told me how to recognize a duck. He said, "If I am in a forest near a lake and come across a little creature that looks like a duck, walks like a duck, quacks like a duck, has feathers like a duck and smells like a duck, chances are I am looking at a duck!"

The story illustrates to the client that the view of reality, "I am not an alcoholic," doesn't fit with the picture that he or she has just painted. This procedure helps the alcoholic focus upon the matter of denial but also clearly communicates that I am not there to hurt or put down, but rather to help. Help means coming to grips with the client's disease process and orienting the client towards a more realistic perception of reality that will eventually facilitate sobriety and positive behavioral change.

Often, as a result of this kind of interaction a working therapeutic alliance is formed, distortions can be evaluated critically by the client-therapist team, and sobriety can be initiated and maintained. Counselors who confront their clients in a warm, caring, nurturant manner, uniformly do better with their clients than counselors who do not have this skill. Dr. Forrest stresses this point throughout his book. This book provides very important and helpful guidelines for all clinicians who are actively involved in treating alcoholic clients. It will be helpful for most counselors to re-read this book from time to time.

Arthur P. Knauert, M.D.
American Psychiatric Assoc. Comm.
on Alcoholism and Drug Abuse.

PREFACE

This book is for therapists and clinicians who are actively involved in the psychotherapeutic treatment of alcoholic patients. Effective confrontation strategies are basic to the successful psychotherapeutic treament of the alcoholic. However, most psychotherapists who work with alcoholics experience a plethora of difficulties as they attempt to utilize confrontation techinques in their treatment relationships.

The issues of when to confront, therapeutic styles of confrontation, patient responses to confrontation, and effective as well as psychonoxious confrontation strategies are discussed. Unlike other publications which deal with the general topic of "confrontation in psychotherapy," the focus of this work is confrontation in psychotherapy with **alcoholics.**

Alcoholics and substance abusing patients consistently present special difficulties when they are seen in extended psychotherapy. These individuals can be very difficult to treat. The alcoholic is often angry, uncommitted to the treatment process and very confrontive toward the therapist.

Psychotherapists tend to be warm, supportive, passive and reluctant to use direct confrontation oriented interventions in their treatment efforts with alcoholics. However, some therapists are consistently angry, manipulative, exploitive and pathologically confrontive in their "therapeutic" relationships with alcoholics. These treatment issues and therapists dilemmas are explored.

xiii

Confrontation techniques appear to be basic to virtually all systems of counseling and psychotherapy. Effective and rational confrontation techniques evolve from a productive therapeutic alliance and encompass the therapist's ability to provide high level facilitative conditions as a part of the confrontation process. Psychonoxious confrontation techniques generally evolve from the counter-transference distortions of the psychotherapist.

Following a brief introduction which touches upon the history of confrontation techniques in therapy are sections which provide the reader with a definition of confrontation in psychotherapy, facilitative confrontation techniques, sources of therapeutic gain, and possible psychonoxious factors in psychotherapy with alcoholic patients.

Alcohol addiction and problem drinking are major health and social problems throughout the world. It is only in recent years that we have collectively concerned ourselves with the treatment of alcoholics and problem drinkers. Hopefully, this book will enhance the therapeutic skills and contribute to the armamentarium of counselors and psychotherapists who work with alcoholics and problem drinkers.

GGF, May 1982

Confrontation
in psychotherapy
with the alcoholic

Chapter 1

Introduction

Psychotherapists and counselors, indeed most behavioral scientists in the "helping professions," have minimized the use of confrontation techniques in psychotherapy (Adler and Myerson, 1973; Bratter, 1975, 1979; Forrest, 1979b). Individuals in treatment seem to have been viewed as fragile, weak, and manifesting very little "ego strength" (Strupp, 1973; Forrest, 1979b). Unfortunately, the psychotherapy patient, in an almost across-the-board fashion, appears to have been perceived in this manner by most professional and paraprofessional change agents.

As a result of this stereotyping of the patient as "fragile," clinicians and psychotherapists have been reluctant to use confrontation techniques in their clinical relationships. Confronting "brittle," inadequate, already overwhelmed patients within the confines of the psychotherapy or counseling has been equated with psychonoxious treatment, decompensation, and iatrogenic outcome phenomena (Yalom, 1970). Admittedly, these are very real clinical concerns for all of us involved in the helping professions.

It is only within the past few years that behavioral scientists, most notably psychotherapists and research psychotherapists, have begun to evaluate confrontation techniques with any real degree of interest and enthusiasm. The literature clearly suggests that confrontation, as a particular dimension of effective psychotherapy with a broad range of patient types, is only now beginning to receive significant attention (Adler and Myerson, 1973; Bratter, 1976, 1979; Emrick, 1979).

It is interesting to speculate about the reasons for this. Certainly, the sixties and early seventies were an era marked by confrontation for the American collective. Peach demonstrations, campus turmoil, the Vietnam War, racial disturbances, police brutality, intercity riots, and the violent activities of numerous revolutionary groups were central to the process of confrontation which the "average" citizen experienced. Surely psychotherapists and evolving philosophies or systems of psychotherapeutic treatment and behavioral change were affected by this confrontation. In fact, it was just at this point that psychotherapists and behavior scientists began an active and clinically relevant exploration of the use of confrontation in psychotherapy.

We live in an ever increasingly action-oriented time and culture. Presently, our psychotherapies and strategies of psychotherapy reflect this culture (Forrest, 1978). Encounter groups, primal therapy, marathon groups, gestalt techniques, behavioral modification techniques, RET and sensitivity training experiences are all generally confrontation oriented. Moreover, these treatment approaches are in large measure predicated upon initiating or facilitating instant change.

In spite of our current and emerging interest in confrontation strategies in psychotherapy, we should recognize that confrontation is a part of all effective systems of counseling and psychotherapy. Classical

psychoanalysis, analytically-oriented psychotherapy, client-centered therapy, reality therapy, RET, existential systems of treatment, and the other "schools" of counseling and psychotherapy have all incorporated confrontation techniques in the treatment relationship (Glasser, 1965, 1976; Patterson, 1966; Ellis, 1979). However, the method of confrontation, the frequency of employment, and the rationale behind this treatment strategy differs in theory and practice among the various systems of counseling and psychotherapy. Rather obviously, the issue of confrontation in psychotherapy is exceedingly complex and multifaceted.

However, the complexity of the problem of utilizing effective confrontation techniques in therapy can be reduced if we 1) discuss what is meant by confrontation, 2) examine facilitative confrontation techniques and sources of therapeutic gain, and 3) explore the psychonoxious processes associated with confrontation. The focus of this book will be limited to these areas.

Chapter 2

Definitions of Confrontation

Attempting to define confrontation as a particular strategy of intervention employed by the psychotherapist within the confines of the psychotherapy relationship is a difficult task (Adler and Myerson, 1973). A plethora of communication problems actively impede our efforts to accurately define confrontation within the context of the therapist-patient relationship. Moreover, what constitutes confrontation or a strategy of confrontation for one therapist may or may not be interpreted as such by another therapist.

Beyond this, what the therapist intends as a direct confrontation may, in fact, not be perceived by the patient as confrontation. At the other end of the continuum, the psychotherapist's attempts at clarification, reflection, and interpretation may be perceived by the patient as potent or threatening confrontations.

Indeed, it is difficult to construct a functional and meaningful definition of confrontation in psychotherapy. However, it is possible to operationally define

the broad parameters of confrontation as a treatment technique within the confines of effective psychotherapy.

Directs Attention

Confrontation explicitly implies force. Confrontation also strongly suggests activity and a focusing of the sensory apparatus of the total human organism in a particular area. With specific reference to the psychotherapy relationship, confrontation describes the methods employed by a therapist to direct the patient's attention upon a particular aspect of his or her self-system. This includes the total aggregate of affective, cognitive, and behavioral dimensions of the patient's self-system.

Focuses on Self-System

A more implicit aspect of confrontation in psychotherapy has to do with developing the patient's ability to focus upon those aspects of the self-system which have been elevated to conscious or preconscious levels by virtue of the work accomplished during earlier stages of the psychotherapeutic process.

Provides Feedback

It is quite apparent that confrontation, as a tool employed by a psychotherapist, is multidimensional in scope and purpose (Myerson, 1973). One important dimension of confrontation is to provide the patient with direct interpersonal feedback relative to the therapist's perception of the patient's affective state, life style, and behavior. Such feedback can be past, present, or future oriented.

Emphasizes Learning

Another significant aspect of confrontation helping the patient to more accurately focus upon himself or herself is that of learning. In this sense, confrontation techniques can be viewed as teaching devices (Mann, 1973). By confronting the patient interpersonally, the therapist, in a very real and direct fashion, teaches the patient to attend to specific behaviors, fantasy ideation, affective states, adjustment styles, and symbolic processes. Such a therapeutic manipulation enables the patient to better understand various self-oriented behaviors and psychodynamic processes.

Stresses Reality

In contrast to the utilization of clarification, reflection, and interpretation techniques, confrontation forcefully and actively exposes the patient to the reality of his or her behaviors and adjustment style as experienced and perceived by the therapist.

An Ingredient of Therapy

Thus far, I have not integrated the role and definition of confrontation techniques in working with alcoholic patients. While the remainder of the text will encompass this matter, it should be pointed out that any definition of confrontation in psychotherapy and rehabilitation work with alcoholic patients must emphasize the utility of confrontation in dealing with avoidance oriented defenses. Alcoholic persons avoid and deny many realities associated with their behaviors, feelings, cognitions and life styles. However, it must be

noted that confrontation techniques do not constitute a complete system of effective counseling and psychotherapy for the patient.

Confrontation is but one ingredient in effective psychotherapy. Likewise, confrontation is only one tool in the psychotherapist's armamentarium (Forrest, 1982).

Chapter 3

Facilitative Techniques

Effective confrontation techniques in psychotherapy with alcoholic patients in both individual and group settings must incorporate high levels of non-possessive warmth, empathy, and genuineness upon the part of the therapist (Forrest, 1975, 1978, 1979a; Scott, 1979; Truax and Carkhuff, 1967). In the absence of therapist care, concern, and involvement, confrontations all too frequently produce iatrogenic effects of varying significance (Truax and Carkhuff, 1967).

Therapist Genuineness

With regard to the essential ingredients of successful therapy, therapist genuineness or authenticity is the most fundamental. Genuineness is defined as "the therapist's ability to be open to his own experience within the therapeutic encounter and to honestly express these feelings to the patient. More simply, the therapist is a real person; he or she wears no facade, expresses feelings and experiences to the patient within the therapeutic encounter, and makes every effort to relate in a personally relevant manner within this context" (Forrest, 1978).

Therapist Non-Possessive Warmth

A second variable in this therapeutic triad is therapist communication of non-possessive warmth for the patient. Basically, this concept relates to "the therapist's warm acceptance of the patient (both experiences and feelings) without any conditions. The therapist accepts what is, rather than being concerned with what should be. The failures and depressions of the patient, as well as successes, are shared by the therapist. It has been assserted in the literature that warmth is a precondition for the therapist to accurately perceive the inner feelings and experiences of the patient, as well as a precondition for the patient's trust and self-exploration" (Forrest, 1978).

Therapist Empathy

The third ingredient within the successful psychotherapeutic encounter is that of accurate empathic understanding. Accurate empathy refers to "the ability of a therapist to be both affectively and cognitively attuned to what the patient is currently feeling and experiencing and to communicate to the patient an understanding of these feelings. Furthermore, the therapist who is accurately empathic will explore the more latent cues expressed by voice, posture and content" (Forrest, 1978).

Mutual Understanding

Effective psychotherapeutic transactions must encompass a mutual understanding and awareness of the realness of these facilitative conditions. Our level and style of communication in psychotherapy must remain at

a level of concreteness which allows for mutual comprehension, meaning, and understanding.

Parataxic Confrontation Styles

Alcoholic individuals becoming engaged in a psychotherapy relationship have led a life style in which significant others have perpetually confronted them in a most hurtful way (Ackerman, 1978). A very important feature in the life of the alcoholic is the consistently parataxic manner in which they have been confronted. Generally speaking, the on-going forms of confrontation which the alcoholic has been subjected to and has learned to direct at others, are antithetical to the facilitative confrontations of the psychotherapist. Confrontations by the parents of alcoholic patients, step-parents, grandparents, close relatives, friends, and significant others are likely to have been permeated with anger, rage, vengeance, and destruction.

As a result of these past inappropriate confrontations, many alcoholics have learned to be pathologically confrontive in their interpersonal relations. Some alcoholic persons feel that they have to "attack, confront and destroy or be themselves attacked and destroyed." They fear annihilation by the confrontations of significant others.

The therapist must be able to demonstrate a healthy degree of liking and caring for his or her alcoholic patients. This will enable the therapist to confront the alcoholic on a consistent basis within an emotional framework characterized by trust, mutual concern, and other affective and cognitive dimensions central to the process of effective psychotherapy. Corrective emotional experience is a very meaningful methodology for describing the change potential so basic to this model of therapist-patient interaction.

As the therapist confronts the alcoholic patient according to this model, one very significant by-product is the breakdown of the patient's pathological confrontation style. Modification of the alcoholic patient's abrasive, aggressive, and overly confrontive presentation of self, in the interpersonal context, is important for long-term sobriety and productive daily living.

The overly confrontive alcoholic is operating in terms of his or her avoidance defense system. When the patient no longer relies upon over-determined defensive measures, interpersonal living becomes easier and more enjoyable.

It must be remembered that the pathology of alcohol addiction is interpersonal in nature, and as such the modification of this distorted pattern of adjustment is contingent upon the patient's ability to change and learn more effective interpersonal behaviors. Change in one area of adjustment and living often initiates or synergizes growth in other areas of interpersonal and intrapersonal living.

Facilitative confrontation strategies with alcoholic patients take place after the patient and therapist have established a meaningful relationship. Direct confrontations and verbal assaults against the patient during the early stages of therapeutic treatment frequently precipitate premature termination and obvious attempts by the patient to flee from treatment. For the patient, this amounts to a re-experiencing of all the emotional hurt, rejection, and pain experienced at the hands of parents, parental imagos and significant others. Preconsciously and unconsciously, the patient understands very well the ultimate pathology and "craziness" inherent in the therapist's utilization of premature, high-impact confrontations.

After the patient has learned to trust the therapist and knows that the therapist is committed to the task of facilitating helpful change and growth, then and only

then, is the patient in a position to meaningfully incorporate the confrontations of the psychotherapist in a manner conducive to integration, synthesis, and thus behavioral and possibly characterological change.

Chapter 4

Confrontation Oriented Sources of Therapeutic Gain

As is the case of all addictions and alloplastic disorders, alcoholism and problem drinking are denial and avoidance oriented adjustment dynamisms (Blane, 1968; Forrest, 1980). The initial and perhaps the most difficult task of the psychotherapist involved in the treatment of alcoholic patients is that of breaking down the system of denial and avoidance which these individuals manifest.

Alcoholism as Defense

From a therapeutic standpoint, it is most efficacious to initially deal with the pathology of the alcoholic's avoidance defenses through direct confrontation. Denial and avoidance defenses play a central role in the patient's relationship and living dilemmas.

Without exception, every alcoholic patient becoming involved in a psychotherapy or counseling relationship initially rejects the reality of his or her alcoholism (Knauert, 1979). In spite of glib verbalizations to the effect of "I know I'm an alcoholic," such individuals during the early stages of treatment preconsciously and unconsciously deny or reject the fact of their addiction. The

patient who has been involved in Alcoholics Anonymous, group therapy, or other treatments, and achieved limited periods of sobriety of perhaps a year's duration or more only to "fall off the wagon" again, has never resolved the pathology of his or her preconscious and unconscious denial of addiction.

A Paradox

The paradoxical bipolarity of the alcoholic character structure is such that every addicted individual knows experientially, at the point of psychotherapeutic engagement, that he or she is addicted. External denial of this reality, often operational for years prior to seeking treatment, is predicated upon the alcoholic's infantile and primitive system of defenses.

Strategies of Therapeutic Intervention

Successful psychotherapeutic resolution of the alcoholic denial dynamism must incorporate: (1) accepting the reality of addiction at the various levels of consciousness and experience, (2) developing a basic understanding and acceptance of the significant contributing interpersonal and intrapersonal variables in the developmental history of the individual and his or her particular addiction process, and (3) learning and relearning the data included in these initial two steps, to the extent that the individual becomes capable of actualizing meaningful and rewarding long-term behavioral alternatives to drinking (Wellman, 1978).

Effecting or initiating these steps frequently begins with the therapist's confrontation "you are an alcoholic" (Forrest, 1978, 1979b). All of the alcoholic's avoidance

oriented defenses require rather direct and systematic confrontation by the therapist.

Obviously, within this context we are dealing with the total character structure of the alcoholic. In this respect, therapeutic and rehabilitation work with addicted or chemically dependent patients requires more direct and potent doses of confrontive behavior upon the part of the therapist than is the case with other clinical populations.

While confrontation techniques are an important aspect of psychotherapeutic work with borderline patients (Kernberg, 1975, 1976) and depressed patients, confrontation strategies are utilized more intermittently and with more caution in the therapeutic management of these disorders. There can be ample clinical justification for this situation. The borderline states, the more schizoid adjustment styles, and the depressive syndromes, all represent clinical conditions in which the reality operations of the individual are significantly impaired in a fashion conducive to periodic decompensation and regression. The impact of the therapist's confrontations can readily facilitate regressive phenomena with these patients. In spite of the apparent overwhelmed state of the ego of most alcoholic patients entering psychotherapeutic treatment, these individuals simply do not tend to decompensate or become floridly psychotic.

Avoid Being a Patsy

For the most part, alcoholics have led confrontation oriented life styles. In part, this explains why therapist confrontations effect or facilitate few massive regressions. This also relates to the effectiveness of confrontation in psychotherapy with alcoholics. Therapists and counselors who are unable to confront addicted patients relative to

their externalizations and avoidance behaviors (denial, distortion, and projection) soon find themselves assuming a therapeutic role of "patsy" (Steiner, 1971).

While such a therapist-patient relationship may be tolerable for both parties during the early stages of the treatment process, rarely in my experience is such a therapeutic alliance conducive to the resolution of the patient's addiction and other problems. Although we have tended to focus upon the problem of denial relative to alcohol addiction, it should be emphasized that the adjustment style of the alcoholic is characterized by a diffuse and pervasive system of avoidance defenses (Forrest, 1978a). Confrontation is a primary psychotherapeutic method for managing and resolving the avoidance type of character armoring.

Internal Conflict

When we use confrontation techniques in psychotherapy with alcoholic patients we are attempting to induce internal conflict. However, the alcoholic patient tends to enter psychotherapy or rehabilitation programs as a result of forces external to the self (Kanuert, 1979; Forrest, 1978, 1979b). These forces are usually the threat of losing a spouse, family, job, or court action (Ackerman, 1978).

Rarely does the alcoholic wish to terminate his or her addiction process at the more primitive levels of consciousness and awareness. Paradoxically, the life style of externalization has reached a state of collapse or impending collapse by the time the patient reaches the psychotherapist's office. What has seemingly worked for the alcoholic, although not well at all in reality, has now become an experiental hell for the addicted person. At this point, the alcoholic is quite likely to be bewildered,

and does not know what to do except to drink. The alcoholic has for many years over-learned drinking as a panacea problem solving technique.

At this juncture, the alcoholic is more susceptible and vulnerable to our confrontations than perhaps at any other time (Forrest, 1979b). Externalization, as an avoidance defense, life style and salient maintenance factor in the alcoholic's self-system has become partially, if not totally, dysfunctional at the point of treatment engagement.

It is only through an increased ability to internalize, rather than externalize, that the alcoholic gains the ability to terminate his or her addiction and change in other significant areas of living.

Fosters Self-Awareness

Confronting alcoholic patients within the confines of the psychotherapy relationship facilitates self-awareness and internalization. This is a painful process for the alcoholic.

Insist on Sobreity

It is imperative that the psychotherapist require the alcoholic patient to be sober at therapy sessions (Forrest, 1978; Knauert, 1979). While this may seem rather elementary, it must be stressed that confronting alcoholic patients can only be effectively accomplished when the patient is sober. In order to learn how to internalize more effectively, the alcoholic must be confronted in therapy while sober.

Inducing internal conflict is a therapeutic methodology by which we attempt to break down the avoidance defenses, and thus the externalization style of the

alcoholic. While the alcoholic has experienced a significant degree of internal conflict, he or she has pathologically learned to deal with this conflict by avoidance and externalization maneuvers. These maneuvers represent neurotic and pathological solutions to internal dissonance. It is imperative that the addicted individual, through the medium of the psychotherapeutic relationship, learn to internalize and work through his or her internal conflicts in a meaningful fashion conducive to positive behavioral change.

Therapy Can Be Painful

Growth is very frequently accompanied by pain. Pain and concomitant growth are related to the productive, on-going confrontations of the psychotherapist.

As alluded to earlier, as a group alcoholic patients tend to be perceived by psychotherapists as rather abrasive. This unfavorable impression of alcoholics stems in large part from the confrontative parameters of the addicted individual's behavioral repertoire. The alcoholic has simply led a confrontation oriented life style (Zinberg, 1973).

Assertive, aggressive, and confrontation oriented interpersonal transactions play a significant part in the interpersonal process of becoming addicted. While the scope, impact, and style of confrontation within the individual alcoholic's life history may vary considerably, this dynamism significantly relates to the psychopathology of every alcoholic.

The Therapist

It is important for therapists to realize that each addicted individual has a unique intrapersonal and interpersonal history which encompasses the learning and, indeed, overlearning of maladaptive confrontation oriented interpersonal behaviors.

As the therapeutic alliance begins to unfold into a neurotic transference relationship, the patient's pathological style of confrontation becomes manifest. The inadequate, markedly passive, "milk-toast" alcoholic patient has problems with confrontation which differ behaviorally and psychodynamically from those of the overly aggressive, assertive, and abrasive addicted patient. Nevertheless, both of these individuals experience significant difficulties in the process of daily living as a result of their confrontation oriented behaviors. How the therapist deals with the alcoholic patient's pathologic style of confrontation affects the development and maintenance of a therapeutic alliance and contributes to the process of affecting patient behavioral change. This is but one dynamic aspect of a successful resolution of the transference neurosis with alcoholic patients.

Confrontation as a relating style is not a typical part of a therapist's basic character structure, let alone an esteemed ingredient in his or her therapeutic armamentarium (Shapiro, 1973). However, in the absence of a learned ability to tolerate this form of interpersonal relating, a psychotherapist will not long function effectively with alcoholic patients.

Alcoholic patients, in a pathologically overdetermined manner, generally relate to the therapist's confrontations as indicators of personal involvement and concern (Knauert, 1979). The pathology basic to such a position does not necessarily negate the reality factors frequently operational in such a perceptual and cognitive

stance upon the part of the patient. In reality, we find very often that, at the point that treatment begins, the patient's spouse and family, friends and employer, and significant others have given up or detached themselves from the patient. This movement away from the patient by significant others is often accompanied with such verbalizations as "go ahead and drink yourself to death" and "you might as well go ahead and kill yourself" (Forrest, 1979b). The therapist's confrontations at a very basic level mean to the patient that another human being still cares enough to interact and become interpersonally involved with him or her.

Hope, a renewed feeling that things can get better, and similar sources of gain are very much a part of the therapist's confrontations at various other levels of the patient's awareness. Thus, therapist confrontation forms the cement of the therapeutic alliance. In the absence of the therapist's ability to help the alcoholic patient, frequently accomplished via the medium of confrontation, suicidal acting-out or other more desperate symbolic cries for help often become a behavioral reality (Forrest, 1979b).

Chapter 5

Psychonoxious Factors Associated With Confrontation

Infrequently, the psychotherapist confronts the alcoholic out of a sense of personal anger and resentment. Some psychotherapists passively absorb the aggressive confrontations of their alcoholic patients. Many competent therapists come to avoid alcoholic patients as a result of their confrontation style and behavior. Characterologically, the alcoholic patient is angry, aggressive and a manipulator. It is of extreme importance to be aware that the alcoholic experiences marked interpersonal difficulties with authority figures (Bratter, 1979).

All of these matters can prove difficult for the psychotherapist. If the therapist is to establish a productive therapeutic alliance with the alcoholic patient he must be able to tolerate these abrasive and often threatening behaviors. In order to do this, the therapist must actively deal with the patient's manipulative, angry and exploitive behaviors. Confrontation is one significant tool in the therapist's interpersonal repertoire for helping accomplish this task.

Therapist-Alcoholic Relationships

In many respects, therapeutic relationships with alcoholic patients prove extremely taxing for the therapist (Bratter, 1979; Forrest, 1979b; Knauert, 1979). As the therapist continually confronts the chinks in the alcoholic patient's character armor and defense system, a working therapeutic alliance is developed. This process accounts for the resolution of the addiction process, as well as the other more basic parataxic processes genetic to the alcoholic adjustment mode.

The establishment of a productive therapeutic alliance is contingent upon the therapist's ability to confront the alcoholic patient with the real feelings and perceptions which the patient stirs in him. Anger, hostility, and other related affective states, tend to be viewed as negative manifestations of countertransference. Nonetheless these are very real matters with which the therapist must personally deal with within the confines of the therapeutic encounter.

When the therapist denies and distorts these personal feelings, he or she reinforces patient pathology and eventually precipitates a therapeutic impasse. Therapists who scotomize their reactions to patient confrontations soon terminate their therapeutic work with alcoholics. Confrontation thus becomes a significant dynamic with regard to the dyadic interations of both therapist and patient vis-a-vis the psychotherapeutic encounter.

Reality Issues in The Therapeutic Relationship

Reality issues pose a particular area of clinical relevance in the psychotherapeutic treatment of the alcoholic patient (Glasser, 1965; Forrest, 1979b). Gross reality disturbances of the more schizophrenic types are not central to the adjustment style of the vast majority of

alcoholics. The reality oriented pathology of the alcoholic relates to the avoidance defense mechanisms discussed earlier. Confrontation strategies can be employed by the psychotherapist to help the alcoholic patient deal more effectively with basic reality operations.

Pathological reality distortion is psychogenically related to basic identity confusion. The deprivation oriented infancy and childhood of the alcoholic serves to create a self-system deplete of basic feelings of self-worth, personal esteem, a sense of personal adequacy and a consolidated identity (Forrest, 1982). The alcoholic systematically learns to feel inferior, inadequate, and develops a failure identity (Forrest, 1978). The developmental process of learning to feel worthless, inadequate, and a "nobody" is extremely painful. Thus, the alcoholic learns to distort or change as much of this unpleasant reality as possible. Helping the alcoholic face the painful realities of the past and present are difficult tasks for the therapist. Therapists who avoid these matters will not be successful in their treatment relationships. Additionally, therapist behaviors of this type are potentially very destructive.

Narcissistic Dimensions of the Therapeutic Relationship

The narcissistic dimensions of the alcoholic character structure (Forrest, 1979c), self-centeredness or outright meglomania, and power fantasy ideation all serve to obfuscate the patient's feelings of interpersonal and intrapersonal impotence. Confronting the alcoholic patient within the confines of the therapeutic encounter, at appropriate times, about the origins and rationale for such distortions enables the patient to eventually establish a reality oriented identity with which she or he can feel relatively better about in the absence of intoxication.

Rather obviously, reality issues span a far greater segment of the psychotherapy relationship with alcoholics. Confronting the alcoholic with our perceptions and interpretations of reality within the context of a productive therapeutic alliance provides the patient with an opportunity for experiential learning, modeling (Bandura, 1969), and thus effects a corrective emotional experience. Just as the sources of gain derived from the psychotherapy relationship are multifaceted and extremely difficult to identify in any cause and effect fashion, so is the role and impact of confrontation strategies in psychotherapy tremendously multivariant in scope and effect.

Perhaps at best I have hit upon a few of the major touchstones which this singular dynamic of the psychotherapy relationship has to offer in the way of facilitating behavior change. Hopefully, the reader will appreciate the complexities and lacunae so fundamental to this matter.

Controlled Confrontation Strategies

Very personal, high impact, premature confrontations, as mentioned earlier, tend to precipitate patient movement away from the therapist and the treatment relationship. However, in rehabilitation and psychotherapeutic work with alcoholic patients, "controlled" confrontations are essential during the initial treatment sessions (Forrest, 1979b). Such "controlled" confrontations, employed early in the psychotherapy relationship, set the groundwork for the eventual establishment of a productive therapeutic alliance. A controlled confrontation simply refers to the therapist's providing the patient with feedback which conveys a point of emphasis, usually a matter of feeling or opinion upon

the part of the therapist which is somewhat dissonant with the self-perceptions of the patient.

For example, a confrontation during the later stages of the psychotherapeutic treatment of an alcoholic patient might well take the form of "every time you've attempted to be a social drinker, you've failed miserably, and now when you tell me again that you think you're ready to make another attempt at social drinking—I honestly wat to say to you: "a very real part of you still wants to remain actively alcoholic." By contrast, during *initial* therapeutic contacts, confrontation might be expressed by stating: "At this point I understand you're feeling that you can do it on your own (achieve and maintain sobriety), but in my experience it very, very rarely ever works out that way." Providing the patient with this form of confrontation oriented feedback early in the treatment relationship does not threaten the patient or precipitate negative affects conducive to fleeing from treatment. On the contrary, such controlled confrontations communicate to the patient a sense of the therapist's honesty, authenticity and a willingness to work with the patient on his or her problems. This stance lets the patient know that the therapist will not allow herself or himself to be "conned" into the role of a patsy (Steiner, 1971).

Patient Reactions to Confrontation

All too frequently psychotherapists victimize themselves and the psychotherapy relationship by assuming passive roles. These therapists are easily conned and manipulated by the patient (Forrest, 1979b; Knauert and Davidson, 1979). While a few alcoholic patients will terminate treatment in the face of early controlled confrontations, most will not.

The therapist must realize that addicted individuals are often not motivated to endure the struggles and pain so basic to the psychotherapy relationship (Bratter, 1973; 1979). In this sense, the response of the patient to early controlled confrontations may be viewed as a barometer of patient readiness and ability to make an on-going commitment to the psychotherapeutic process. The ability of the therapist to utilize controlled confrontations effectively is closely associated with successful treatment outcome.

Very often the therapist must learn through experience that his or her confrontations will not, in reality or symbolically, "kill" the patient or the therapeutic alliance. As with interpretations, reflections and various other psychotherapeutic techniques of effective psychotherapy, the therapist learns most effectively as a result of direct clinical experience.

Sources of Therapist Countertransference

A basic psychodynamic consideration in therapeutic work with alcoholic patients, as with other patients, has to do with our own countertransference distortions related to rescuing or saving the patient (Forrest, 1979b; Knauert and Davidson, 1979). The alcoholic entering treatment is depressed, overwhelmed, and literally "begging for help." As such, the alcoholic sets the therapist up for assuming a rescuing position. Indeed, the alcoholic may well need healthy rescuing at this point, possibly to include detoxification and other medical forms of direct intervention.

In the event that such "rescuing" is clinically appropriate, the therapist must soon after confront the alcoholic patient with his or her responsibility in choosing to drink or not to drink. Many alcoholism counselors

negate the significance of this therapeutic issue. As a result, such counselors and therapists tend to construct highly dependent relationships with their patients in which superficial sobriety and behavioral change upon the part of the patient is pathologically contingent upon the on-going rescuing transactions of the therapist. Ultimately, such a psychotherapy alliance suffers an irreversible impasse. In fact, the alcoholic patient may be killed by this form of on-going transaction. The therapist must actively and consistently confront the patient with the matter of behaving responsibly, to include drinking per se. This is an area in which all alcoholics experience chronic difficulty (Knauert, 1979).

This is a sensitive area for the psychotherapist. Premature, direct confrontations to this effect can be interpreted by the patient to mean that the therapist is either disinterested in the patient or that he or she lacks the ability to be of help. It is through the creation of a productive therapeutic alliance that the patient acquires the ability to behave more responsibly and effectively.

We must bear in mind that few alcoholic patients fully appreciate or grasp the reality of this situation during the initial stages of the psychotherapeutic process. Thus, we must openly discuss these matters in order that the patient might not terminate treatment prematurely as a result of not evidencing immediate marked behavioral and symptomatic change.

As touched upon earlier, psychonoxious confrontation styles or transactions evolve from the countertransference distortions of the therapist. Anger, rejection, and patient dislike form the nuclear core of the therapist's pathological confrontations. As a result of the alcoholic's personal confrontation style and iconoclastic attitudes, the katogogic or neurotic trends of the psychotherapist are exacerbated (McGahee, 1978). It becomes apparent during even the intital treatment sessions that many addicted

patients have very little desire to change their addictive life style. Thus, from the onset of the treatment process they may ultimately wish to defeat the therapist.

This is the case with the spectrum of alloplastic disorders. As treatment progresses, psychotherapists and counselors who deny or otherwise fail to fully appreciate the clinical relevance of this dynamic find themselves becoming more and more angry with their addicted patients. Iatrogenic confrontation strategies tend to evolve from the therapist's feelings of frustration, anger, and at times, poorly controlled rage (Forrest, 1979b).

This counter-productive state of affairs most frequently involves counselors and therapists who have had little experience in the therapeutic management of addicted or chemically dependent individuals. Countertransference distortions very often stem from therapist-patient transactions. The therapist, in a pathological manner, may reject the patient in the face of a massive regression to drinking and concomitant "craziness."

Rescuing

During the intitial stages of treatment, the therapist assumes the role of a good parent ego-introject and attempts to rescue the patient from his or her addiction and from presumed persecutors. Such a transaction immediately proves rewarding; a "therapeutic honeymoon" for both parties.

In such cases, the alcoholic very often becomes intoxicated again. The reality of "ups and downs" in the psychotherapeutic management of the alcoholic involves both intoxication and sobriety (Forrest, 1980). After patients have experienced numerous slips, therapists understandably experience a sense of frustration. They can easily experience disillusionment and become angry.

As these countertransference factors become increasingly significant and operational, the therapist unwittingly sabotages the therapeutic alliance vis-a-vis active movement into the role of a primary persecutor (Forrest, 1979b). Such a transaction during early treatment typically involves the therapist as one who victimizes and scapegoats the patient.

The therapist caught up in the roles of "rescuer-scapegoater-persecutor" typically has very few confrontations with the patient during early treatment. Furthermore, there is likely to be progressive acting-out by the therapist employing direct and blatantly angry confrontations during the later stages of treatment. Eventually, the therapist scapegoats the alcoholic and becomes an active persecutor of the patient. As the therapist assumes the stance of persecutor, the verbal content of the therapist's fantasy ideation is often expressed along the lines of "by God, you will get sober!" At this point the verbal dialogue between the therapist and patient, as well as body language and other expressions neurotically serve to push the patient in the direction of sobriety and behavioral change.

At the juncture of complete therapeutic impasse or rupture in the therapeutic alliance, the therapist typically rejects the patient with angry confrontations which effect in the patient feelings of hopelessness, abandonment, rejection, and a sense that he or she is incapable of constructive change. This form of mutual "giving up" frequently relates to the problem of suicide and suicidal acting-out by alcoholic patients while in psychotherapeutic treatment and following treatment (Forrest, 1979b). At best, this situation in running its course becomes licensure for the patient to remain intoxicated and otherwise dysfunctional.

Therapist Narcissism

Alcoholic patients frequently provoke counter-transference distortions in the therapist related to issues of therapist omnipotence and narcissism (Bratter, 1979; Forrest, 1979c; Knauert and Davidson, 1979). It is true that working with alcoholic patients can be very painful and unrewarding. Therapist over-involvement with the alcoholic must of necessity precipitate feelings of therapeutic impotence and self-doubt in the face of continued or intermittent intoxication and other behavioral "craziness" while in treatment. Outright treatment failures most directly threaten the omnipotent and narcissistic needs of the psychotherapist (Knauert and Davidson, 1979).

In the face of apparent regression or little therapeutic gain, the therapist commonly experiences a personal sense of frustration which enhances the probability of his utilizing confrontation strategies in a distorted manner. The confrontations of the therapist who is personally threatened by his or her apparent lack of success in treating the alcoholic frequently take the form of directives or demands that the patient get better. This type of counterproductive therapeutic relationship represents the example par excellence of an iatrogenic countertransference transaction.

Therapist Responsibility

A fundamental requirement or ground rule in the psychotherapeutic treatment of addicted and chemically dependent patients is that the therapist never accepts responsibility for the patient's addictive behaviors once he or she has entered treatment (Matuschka, 1979). To do so is to set oneself up for therapeutic impasse, which

classically incorporates the utilization of parataxic confrontation strategies upon the part of the psychotherapist. This is a neurotic method for maintaining therapist self esteem, a professional identity of competence, and the other rudiments of a reasonably well integrated self-system. The realization that we simply do not possess the ability to somehow initiate magical cures is a matter which every psychotherapist must personally come to grips with and integrate into our treatment relationships. To fail on this account is to render our confrontation techinques subject to a plethora of countertransference distortions.

Therapist Identify and Security

Many therapists mistakenly react to beliefs that only an alcoholic can treat an alcoholic, or that shrinks don't really know anything about alcoholism. As a result, many therapists in defense of their professional identities initiate direct confrontation maneuvers to dispel these feelings and beliefs of the patient. These maneuvers are psychonoxious.

Again, this is an extremely sensitive area of therapeutic concern which requires appropriate management by the therapist. The therapist who feels compelled to counteract these negative patient sentiments, and attempts to do so by the method of confrontation, is operating out of a pathologically overdetermined countertransference set. Counselors and psychotherapists who are not truly familiar with the modus operandi of the alcoholic frequently experience difficulty as a result of their attempts to, in effect, demonstrate their therapeutic skills. The patient who brings these attitudes and feelings to the treatment situation must be gently

confronted and made aware of the therapist's willingness
to help. This becomes a matter of sensitively utilizing the
technique of confrontation.

SUMMARY

Confrontation strategies are a basic ingredient in all systems of effective counseling and psychotherapy. The actual definition of confrontation, as a psychotherapeutic technique, encompasses a rather broad spectrum of therapist-patient behaviors. In the present context, confrontation is defined as a method by which the psychotherapist attempts to focus or direct the patient's attention upon a particular aspect of his or her self-system. The parameters of what in reality consitutues a confrontation are quite nebulous. More simply, what is meant to be a confrontation upon the part of the therapist may not be interpreted as such by the patient. The supportive attempts of the therapist to clarify, reflect, or interpret may be construed by the patient as threatening confrontations.

Confrontation techniques are essential to effective psychotherapeutic work with alcoholic patients. A primary source of gain provided by this technique is that of resolving the avoidance defense system of the alcoholic. The establishment of a productive therapeutic alliance with addicted and chemically dependent patients is very often contingent upon the therapist's ability to utilize healthy confrontation techniques early and throughout the course of treatment. Psychotherapists who are unable to actualize healthy confrontation strategies with their

addicted patients are either marginally effective in their treatment efforts or they soon divorce themselves from this clinical population. The pathological confrontation style of many alcoholic patients presents a barrier to effective treatment for many counselors and psychotherapists (Forrest, 1979b; Knauert and Davidson, 1979).

Healthy and effective methods of psychotherapeutic confrontation tend to become progressively relevant to the productive treatment relationship. Facilitative confrontations stem from the care and concern of the psychotherapist for his or her patient. Effective confrontations always evolve through the medium of a productive therapeutic alliance. Premature, high impact confrontations by the therapist often result in the patient's fleeing from treatment. This type of confrontation is more appropriate once a productive therapeutic alliance has been established and subsequently reached an impasse. "Controlled" confrontations permeate the work of the psychotherapist and are very much a part of the initial treatment process with chemically dependent patients.

Countertransference distortions are almost without exception basic to the employment of psychonoxious confrontation techinques. In these situations the therapist typically confronts the patient out of feelings of anger and rage. Frequently, this form of counterproductive confrontation stems from an initial "rescuer" transaction upon the part of the therapist which eventually goes sour. The result is a role reversal situation in which the therapist becomes an actual persecutor of the patient. This transactional process, in running its course, is iatrogenic to the degree of precipitating suicidal acting-out on the part of certain alcoholic patients (Forrest, 1979b; Scott, 1979a). The interpersonal style of the alcoholic tends to generate countertransference distortion. The therapist's ability to

personally manage this matter relates to his or her utilization of adaptive confrontation techniques.

BIBLIOGRAPHY

BIBLIOGRAPHY

Ackerman, R. J. *Children of Alcoholics: A Guidebook for Educators, Therapists and Parents.* Learning Publications, Holmes Beach, FL, 1978.

Adler, G. and Myerson, P. G. *Confrontation in Psychotherapy,* Eds. Science House, New York, 1973.

Bandura, A. *Principles of Behavior Modification.* Holt, Rinehart and Wilson, New York, 1969.

Blane, H. T. *The Personality of the Alcoholic: Guises of Dependency.* Harper and Row, New York, 1968.

Bratter, T. E. Confrontation: A Group Psychotherapeutic Orientation with Heroin Addicts. In: Uchtenhagen, A., Battegay, R. and Friedemann, A., Eds. *Group Therapy and Social Environment* (Switzerland: Hans Huber, 1975) p. 360-367.

Bratter, T.E. Confrontation Groups: The Therapeutic Community's Gift to Psychotherapy In: Vanos, P. and Devlin, J., Eds. *Proceedings of the First World Conference on Therapeutic Communities* (Montreal: Potage Press, 1976) p. 164-174.

Bratter, T. E. Responsible Therapeutic Eros: The Psychotherapist Who Cares Enough to Define and Enforce Behavioral Limits with Potentially Suicidal Adolescents. *The Counseling Psychologist.* 5:4(1975a) p. 97-104.

Bratter, T. E. The Psychotherapist as a Twelfth Step Worker in the Treatment of Alcoholism. *Family and Community Health.* Vol. 2, No. 2, August, p. 31-58, 1979.

Ellis, A. Rational Emotive Therapy Training. Lecture presented at Psychotherapy Associates, P.C. Fifth Annual Advanced Treatment and Rehabilitation of the Alcoholic Winter Workshop, Colorado Springs, CO, Feb. 1, 1979.

Emrick, C. D. Perspectives in Clinical Research: Relative Effectiveness of Alcohol Abuse Treatment. *Family and Community Health,* Vol. 2, No. 2, August, p. 71-88, 1979.

Forrest, G. G. *Alcoholism, Narcissism and Psychopathology.* Text in press, 1982.

Forrest, G. G. Alcoholism, Object Relations and Narcissistic Theory. Lecture presented at Psychotherapy Associates, P.C. Fifth Annual Advanced Treatment and Rehabilitation of the Alcoholic Winter Workshop, Colorado Springs, CO, Jan. 29, 1979.

Forrest, G. G. *How to Live with a Problem Drinker and Survive.* Atheneum, New York, 1980.

Forrest, G. G. Negative and Positive Addictions. *Family and Community Health.* Vol. 2, No. 1, May, p. 103-112, 1979a.

Forrest, G. G. Setting Alcoholics up for Therapeutic Failure. *Family and Community Health,* Vol. 2, No. 2, August, p. 59-64, 1979b.

Forrest, G. G. *The Diagnosis and Treatment of Alcoholism.* Charles C. Thomas, Publisher, Springfield, IL, 1975; Rev. 2nd Ed., 1978.

Garner, H. G. *Psychotherapy: Confrontation Problem Solving Technique.* Warren H. Green, Inc., St. Louis, MO, 1970.

Glasser, W. *Reality Therapy.* Harper and Row, New York, 1965.

Glasser, W. *Positive Addiction.* Harper and Row, New York, 1976.

Kernberg, O. *Borderline Conditions and Pathological Narcissism.* Jason Aronson, Inc., New York, 1975.

Kernberg, O. *Object Relations Theory and Clinical Psychoanalysis.* Jason Aronson, Inc., New York, 1976.

Knauert, A.P. The Treatment of Alcoholism in a Community Setting. *Family and Community Health.* Vol. 2, No. 1, May, p. 91-102, 1979.

Knauert, A. P., and Davidson, S. V. Maintaining the Sanity of Alcoholism Counselors. *Family and Community Health.* Vol. 2, No. 2, August, p. 65-70, 1979.

Mann, J. Confrontation as a Mode of Teaching. In: Adler, G. and Myerson, P.G., *Confrontation in Psychotherapy,* Eds., Science House, New York, 1973.

Matuschka, E. Bioenergetic Training. Lecture presented at Psychotherapy Associates, P.C., Fifth Annual Advanced Treatment and Rehabilitation of the Alcoholic Winter Workshop, Colorado Springs, CO, Feb 1, 1979.

Myerson, P. G. The Meaning of Confrontation. In: Adler, G. and Myerson, P. G. *Confrontation in Psychotherapy,* Eds., Science House, New York, 1973.

McGahee, B. Treatment of the Inhibited Neurotic Alcoholic. Lecture presented at Psychotherapy Associates, P.C. Second Annual Southeastern Fall Treatment and Rehabilitation of the Alcoholic Workshop, Savannah, GA, Oct. 1, 1978.

Patterson, C. H. *Theories of Counseling and Psychotherapy.* Harper and Row, New York, 1966.

Scott, E. M. Death and Dying in the Alcoholic. Lecture presented at Psychotherapy Associates, P.C. Fifth Annual Advanced Treatment and Rehabilitation of the Alcoholic Winter Workshop, Colorado Springs, CO, Jan. 30, 1979.

Scott, E. M. Group Psychotherapy with the Alcoholic: Theory and Practice. Lecture presented at Psychotherapy Associates, P.C. Fifth Annual Advanced Treatment and Rehabilitation of the Alcoholic Winter Workshop, Colorado Springs, CO, Jan. 30, 1979.

Shapiro, L. N. Confrontation with the "Real" Analyst. In: Adler, G. and Myerson, P.G., *Confrontation in Psychotherapy,* Eds., Science House, New York, 1973.

Steiner, C. *Games Alcoholics Play.* Grove Press, Inc., New York, 1971.

Strupp, H. H. *Psychotherapy: Clinical, Research and Theoretical Issues.* Jason Aronson, Inc., New York, 1973.

Truax, C. B. and Carkhuff, R. R. *Toward Effective Counseling and Psychotherapy: Training and Practice.* Aldine, Chicago, 1967.

Wellman, L. E. Applied Social Learning Theory in the Treatment of the Alcoholic. Lecture presented at Psychotherapy Associates, P.C. Fifth Annual Advanced Treatment and Rehabilitation of the Alcoholic Winter Workshop, Colorado Springs, CO, Feb. 1, 1979.

Yalom, I. D. *The Theory and Practice of Group Psychotherapy.* Basic Books, Inc., Publishers, New York, 1970.

Zinberg, N. E. The Techniques of Confrontation and Social Class Differences. In: Adler, G. and Myerson, P. G. *Confrontation in Psychotherapy,* Eds., Science House, New York, 1973.

DATE DUE

MR 21 '90			
OC1 7 '90			
JY 11 '91			
DE 29 '92			
SE 30 '93			
DE 12 '98			
OC 28 '03			
DE 11 '03			